HITLER, GOEBBELS, HIMMLER
The Nazi Holocaust Masterminds

Linda Jacobs Altman

REMEMBERING THE HOLOCAUST

Enslow Publishers, Inc.
40 Industrial Road
Box 398
Berkeley Heights, NJ 07922
USA

http://www.enslow.com

Originally published as *The Holocaust, Hitler, and Nazi Germany* in 1999.

Library of Congress Cataloging-in-Publication Data

Altman, Linda Jacobs, 1943– [Holocaust, Hitler, and Nazi Germany]
      Hitler, Goebbels, Himmler : the Nazi Holocaust masterminds / Linda Jacobs Altman.
            pages cm. — (Remembering the holocaust)
      Previously published under the title: The Holocaust, Hitler, and Nazi Germany. Berkeley Heights, NJ : Enslow, © 1999.
      Includes bibliographical references and index.
      ISBN 978-0-7660-6197-2
      1. Holocaust, Jewish (1939–1945)—Juvenile literature. 2. Germany—History—Juvenile literature. 3. Hitler, Adolf, 1889–1945—Juvenile literature. I. Title.
      D804.34.A49 2014
      940.53'18—dc23

                                        2014007025

Future Editions:
Paperback ISBN: 978-0-7660-6198-9
EPUB ISBN: 978-0-7660-6199-6
Single-User PDF ISBN: 978-0-7660-6200-9
Multi-User PDF ISBN: 978-0-7660-6201-6

To Our Readers: We have done our best to make sure all Internet addresses in this book were active and appropriate when we went to press. However, the author and the publisher have no control over and assume no liability for the material available on those Internet sites or on other Web sites they may link to. Comments can be sent by e-mail to comments@enslow.com or to the address on the back cover.

Illustration Credits: Enslow Publishers, Inc., pp. 16, 30; National Archives, pp. 1, 4.

Cover Illustration: National Archives and Records Administration (NARA): Woman in the Sudetenland weeping upon the annexation of the territory to Nazi Germany.

CONTENTS

Hitler annexed Austria as part of his quest for German "living space."
He received a standing ovation at the Reichstag after announcing his
"peaceful" acquisition of the country.

Introduction

MANDATE FOR MURDER

O n April 11, 1945, American troops liberated the Nazi concentration camp at Buchenwald. These soldiers had faced death many times. They had known the misery of twentieth-century warfare. None of that had prepared them for the horrors of Buchenwald: "No sooner had we passed the barbed wire gate than a nauseating stench reached our nostrils. But what we saw was even worse," recalled a soldier of General George Patton's Third Army.

> There were dead bodies all around the camp, some lying side by side, others piled upon each other like cordwood. . . . [Further on] beyond the buildings, was a deep pit. It was filled with naked bodies—men, women and children—in all the grotesque positions of death. Someone said that these dead were Jews.[1]

American generals Dwight Eisenhower, Omar Bradley, and George Patton viewed the carnage. General Patton—the

fierce fighter everyone called "Old Blood and Guts"—stumbled away from the death pit and vomited.

General Eisenhower ordered the troops to document everything they saw. He wanted to be sure that nobody could ever dismiss it as "merely . . . propaganda."[2] The troops took pictures and talked to prisoners. In this way, they uncovered one horrifying truth after another.

New words came into the language and old words took on new meanings. In 1944, attorney Ralph Lemkin coined the word *genocide*. It meant the systematic killing of an entire racial, ethnic, political, or religious group. *Holocaust* originally meant mass destruction, especially by fire. After the war, it was used to describe the senseless slaughter that claimed millions of lives.

The saga of the Holocaust begins with Adolf Hitler and the National Socialist German Workers' (Nazi) Party. "Nazi" comes from the first four letters of the German *NAZIonal*. By calling their regime the Third Reich, the Nazis were claiming kinship with great leaders of the German past.

The First Reich was the Holy Roman Empire. The pope laid its foundation in 800. That year, he bestowed the title of Holy Roman Emperor on Charlemagne of the Franks. The Second Reich began in 1871, when Otto von Bismarck unified the German states. It ended in 1918, with Germany's defeat in World War I.

Between the two world wars, Germany experimented with democracy. The Weimar Republic (named after the town where the constitution was written) did not last long. It faltered during the Great Depression that began in 1929. It collapsed altogether when Adolf Hitler came to power.

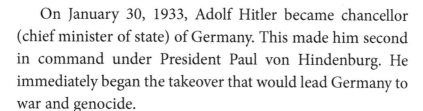

On January 30, 1933, Adolf Hitler became chancellor (chief minister of state) of Germany. This made him second in command under President Paul von Hindenburg. He immediately began the takeover that would lead Germany to war and genocide.

Eleven million people, 6 million of them Jews, perished during the twelve years of the Nazi Reich. Many have doubted that this grim fact could ever be explained or understood. Judaic Studies professors Calvin Goldscheider and Alan S. Zuckerman called the devastation of the Holocaust "unimaginable." The scholars said that its meaning was "beyond the [understanding] of humans."[3] Others, like historian John Weiss, do not agree: "The Holocaust," Weiss wrote, "is unique, but it is not [beyond understanding]."[4] Its causes and effects can be studied and analyzed.

Sooner or later, anyone who studies the Holocaust must confront two questions: How could this have happened in a civilized country, and who is to blame? The search for answers has led to controversy.

Some have placed most of the blame on Adolf Hitler and the Nazi leadership. The opinions of historian Sebastian Haffner are a good example: "After 1933, something like a Führer state [a dictatorship] would probably have come into being even without Hitler. And there probably would have been another war even without Hitler. But not the murder of millions of Jews."[5]

The idea of "no Hitler, no Holocaust"[6] has gone out of favor with most historians. There is a new focus on the role of the unknown, ordinary people. The Nazi leadership planned the Holocaust, but hundreds of ordinary people carried it out. The killing could not have happened without

them. Taken to its limits, the focus on the role of ordinary people in carrying out the Holocaust can lead to what John Weiss calls "bankrupt theories of collective responsibility"[7] (blaming the entire German people).

Most of those who study Nazi Germany believe the truth lies somewhere between the extremes. It is wrong to blame all Germans for the Holocaust. But it is also wrong to blame only Adolf Hitler and the Nazi leadership. Many factors came together at a particular time and place in history. The result was a world war, accompanied by genocide. Learning how and why these horrors came about can perhaps help us ensure that they never happen again.

Chapter 1

BARBARIANS, BELIEVERS, AND TYRANTS

In the second century B.C., the ancestors of modern Germans migrated from Northern Europe, and settled along the borders of the Roman Empire. They were not a single nation, but a group of tribes that shared a common ancestry. They called themselves Theut, meaning simply "the folk" or "the people." The name German comes from Germani, the Roman name for one of the tribes.

After the Western Roman Empire collapsed in the fifth century A.D., the Germans pushed across the Rhine and Danube rivers. They took over Roman territories, but they had no desire to build an empire of their own. They valued personal freedom too much to live by a code of laws.

Government was almost nonexistent, and warfare was a way of life. The Roman historian Tacitus wrote that the Germanic tribes "actually think it tame and stupid to acquire by the sweat of toil what they might win by their blood."[1]

Although the Western Roman Empire was politically dead, some of its culture remained. The Germans mixed it with their own and later added Christianity to the mix. Thus, Christian, German, and Roman elements formed the foundation of German culture.

The Empire Builders

Charlemagne became king of the Franks in 768 and Holy Roman Emperor in 800. Throughout his long reign, he was almost constantly at war, extending the borders of his kingdom.

For all his power, Charlemagne could not sell the idea of an empire to the tribal Germans. They wanted leaders they could see, talk with, and touch. They cared nothing for the faceless politics of empires.[2]

Charlemagne failed to match the grandeur of ancient Rome, but he did accomplish many things. He began to transform the hodgepodge of German law into a consistent legal code. He established a standard currency to build a good foundation for the economy. Then he turned to the Jews for help in building commerce and industry.

Jews had come to Europe in large numbers after the Roman legions laid waste to Palestine in A.D. 135. They made a place for themselves in commerce and finance. Hundreds of Jews answered Charlemagne's call. Some of them found high positions in the royal court. They served as advisors, administrators, and diplomats.

Charlemagne's empire began to fall apart after his death. Princes quibbled among themselves, fought wars at the drop of an insult, and gave only grudging allegiance to each new emperor.

Frederick the Great and the Rise of Prussia

Until the reign of Frederick the Great (ruled 1740–1786), Prussia was an unimportant possession of the state of Brandenburg. It was small, sparsely populated, and lacking in natural resources; yet from this unlikely little domain would come a new German empire.

Brandenburg-Prussia was controlled by a landed aristocracy called *Junkers*. This elite group of twelve thousand to fifteen thousand families lived by a harsh, militaristic code. They glorified combat and regarded warfare as part of "the normal order of the world."[3] Junkers dominated the Prussian military and served in the highest levels of government. As a class, they stood for privilege and power. Frederick insisted that his entire officer corps be Junkers. With their help, he expanded Prussia by conquering neighboring kingdoms. The Prussian Army became known for its ruthlessness. Frederick's method was to attack without warning, striking hard and fast with overwhelming force.

This bold warrior-king did have a softer side. He loved music, art, philosophy, and literature. He surrounded himself with people who shared these interests. Everywhere in Prussia, scholarship and the arts flourished.

Frederick also completed many public improvement projects. He built roads, reclaimed wasteland for agriculture, and expanded industries such as textile manufacture. He strengthened the legal system with centralized courts and forbade torture as a means of questioning people accused of crimes.

In spite of these advances, Frederick's Prussia never ceased to be an autocracy. The king was the final authority on everything. Government agencies were responsible only

to him. He could override their actions at anytime. The common people had no voice.

During the forty-six years of his reign, Frederick the Great transformed Prussia from an unimportant backwater into a powerful state. He did not succeed in unifying the Germanys into a true nation. That task awaited a later ruler.

Napoléon's Europe

On July 14, 1789, Frenchmen stormed the Bastille, a fortress prison in the heart of Paris. To the cry of "Liberty! Equality! Fraternity!"[4] the French Revolution began. It triggered a series of wars that led to the rise of Napoléon Bonaparte.

Beginning in 1799, Napoléon blazed through Europe, shattering all that remained of the Holy Roman Empire. In October 1806, he conquered Prussia. The rest of the German states fell one by one.

For Jews throughout Western Europe, Napoléon's victory meant the beginning of freedom. The Napoléonic code of 1804 provided for Jewish liberation throughout the empire of France. Not only did the Jewish people gain civil rights, the Jewish religion was declared equal to Christianity.

In Germany, hatred of the French conquerors triggered the rise of nationalism. The Germans were stung by the defeats of their fragmented kingdoms. They dreamed of creating a unified German nation founded on the "original spirit, religion, and ways of the *Volk*."[5]

The word *volk* simply means "people," but to German volkists, it came to mean "a tribal unity of blood."[6] The volk were connected to one another and to the land. In that connection was an inborn superiority to so-called lesser races.

In 1813, the German states got their chance to create a new nation. They combined to defeat the French and reclaim their political independence. Freed at last of foreign rule, the German states stood at a crossroads. Down one path was a unified nation; down the other, the old collection of patch-work principalities.

The lure of unity was not yet strong enough to overcome the bickering among princes. At the Congress of Vienna in 1815, the delegates could only agree to form a loose alliance called the German Confederation.

The return of petty princes and weak states was a setback to those who dreamed of a great nation. It was a disaster for minorities in these countries, especially the Jews. Most of the states repealed or severely limited the civil rights that Napoléon had given them.

In 1848, liberal nationalists revolted against the power of the princes. They called for a unified German nation-state, with civil liberties, economic freedom, and a democratic government. Although the liberals could not gather enough support to unseat the princes, they did achieve limited reforms. After the revolt, Prussia established an elected parliament to share power with the king. Prince Otto von Bismarck, the man who would unify Germany and launch the Second Reich, served in this first parliament.

The Rise of Prince Bismarck

Otto von Bismarck was no believer in democracy. He was an autocrat and a Junker who wanted to unify Germany under Prussian rule. His Germany would be a nation of warriors; men who settled disputes on the field of battle, not in the chambers of government. As Bismarck himself once put it,

"the great decisions of the day are not made by parliamentary majorities, but by blood and iron."[7]

This attitude was not unusual by the standards of the time. Warfare was a legitimate way to settle differences, gain political power, or expand territory. For hundreds of years that had been the way of things. A nation would stand or fall on its military skill.

When Bismarck became prime minister of Prussia in 1862, King Wilhelm I was arguing with the parliament over military reform. Wilhelm wanted to expand the Prussian Army, but parliament refused to fund the project. The new prime minister put the problem to rest with his famous *Luckentheorie* (gap theory). This stated that in conflicts between the king and the parliament, the will of the king must prevail. Thus, Wilhelm bypassed parliament and funded military expansion on his own authority.

Bismarck used the larger army to launch three wars to expand Prussian power. In 1864, he sided with Austria in a war to take disputed territory from Denmark. Two years later, he turned on his former ally in a plot to destroy the German Confederation. Bismarck knew that the confederation would fall without Austrian backing. He therefore engineered a war that Austria could not hope to win. In seven weeks of fighting, Prussia defeated Austria. Bismarck promptly dissolved the German Confederation and brought the twenty-two states of northern Germany under Prussian control.

In 1870, Bismarck provoked the third war of unification, this time against France. He then convinced the south German princes that only a unified Germany could protect

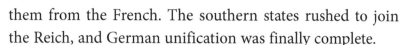

them from the French. The southern states rushed to join the Reich, and German unification was finally complete.

On January 18, 1871, Wilhelm I of Prussia was crowned kaiser (emperor) of the new German Reich. Bismarck became chancellor. The conservative Junkers rejoiced that one of their own had taken the reins of power. However, Bismarck promptly shocked them with a series of reforms. He granted full civil rights to Jews and established universal male suffrage (voting rights) for the lower house of the Reichstag (parliament).

These shrewd reforms won many liberals to Bismarck's cause without actually changing the balance of power in German government. The aristocracy remained in control of the upper house of the Reichstag. There, membership was determined by right of birth, not by election. Democratic principles did not apply.

The Second Reich and the Jews

Jews greeted their emancipation as an invitation into the mainstream of German life. They wanted to be regarded as citizens and patriots who just happened to practice a different religion from the majority of their countrymen: "Their love of and loyalty to the new Germany was beyond question," wrote historian Alexis P. Rubin.

> They entered the professions in large numbers becoming doctors, lawyers, teachers, journalists. They applied their . . . commercial skills to big business which was then [growing] as a result of the Industrial Revolution. They also invested in the stock markets and worked on the exchanges.[8]

This Jewish advance happened at a time of massive social change. The Industrial Revolution was turning Germany

After leading Germany into a series of wars, Otto von Bismarck had succeeded in unifying the German states (shaded) by 1871.

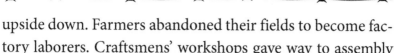

upside down. Farmers abandoned their fields to become factory laborers. Craftsmens' workshops gave way to assembly lines. Science challenged religious authority, turning believers into doubters. People felt dispossessed and uncertain; they had lost their moorings, and they needed someone to blame.

The Jews made the perfect target. They still seemed like foreigners, no matter how well they spoke German or how loudly they proclaimed their German patriotism. Not even Christianized Jews were safe from this new outbreak of hatred. Jews were Jews, people said; they always would be. Jewishness was inescapable. At that point, prejudice began to take a deadly turn into racism.

In 1879, German nationalist Wilhelm Marr wrote a book in which he blamed the Jews for all of Germany's troubles. According to Marr, Jews were constantly scheming for wealth and power. Evil was in their blood. They could not change. They would not be satisfied until they ruled all of Germany.

Marr invented the term *anti-Semitism* (hatred of Jews as a people) to describe his philosophy. In the 1880s, he founded the Anti-Semitic League and began publishing a journal, *German, On Guard!* Again and again, he put forth the message: If Germany did not destroy the Jews, then the Jews would destroy Germany.

"Inherent in Marr's racism of blood was a potential for genocide," wrote John Weiss. "If the Jews were evil, unchangeable, and about to conquer, they must be dragged from their positions in society and rendered harmless; even a Jewish infant was a mortal threat. . . . Marr's was the racism that led to the death camps."[9]

Politics in Bismarck's Germany

Anti-Semitism did not take place in a political vacuum. Jewish rights were grounded in Bismarck's alliance with the liberals. They did not grow out of commitment to human rights as a matter of principle. At heart, Bismarck remained a firm believer in an authoritarian, class-based social order. His methods earned him the nickname "Iron Chancellor."

It was the misfortune of this Iron Chancellor to serve at a time when new political movements challenged old ideas. The Center party and the Social Democrats appeared especially dangerous. The Center party represented Germany's Catholics, whereas the Social Democrats were a working-class party favoring state socialism. Bismarck considered them both *reichsfeinde*, enemies of the Reich. Both parties claimed loyalties that went beyond national borders. In Bismarck's mind, this raised questions of loyalty. Would socialists betray Germany to further their political aims? In a conflict between the Reich and the Roman Catholic Church, where would the Center party stand?

In 1870, with what turned out to be a masterpiece of bad timing, Pope Pius IX tried to expand the church's role in secular (nonreligious) affairs. Citing the authority of Christ himself, Pius declared that the pope was the final authority in disputes with political leaders. The Iron Chancellor would not tolerate this action. He responded with a *Kulturkampf* (cultural struggle). New laws limited the role of the church in matters such as marriage, divorce, and education. The rift between the Catholic Church and the German nation grew dangerously wide. Bismarck held firm until a new pope ruled in the Vatican. Only then did he try to mend relations

with the church. He did this by blaming Jews in the Reichstag for causing the Kulturkampf.

The church was not von Bismarck's only political foe. By 1878, growing working-class support for the Social Democratic party had become worrisome. To counter its appeal, Bismarck tried to take over its issues. He introduced a broad program of social legislation; including health, accident, old-age, and disability insurance. Although these programs were popular with the working class, they did not cut into support for the Social Democrats. In spite of Bismarck's efforts, the party continued to grow.

In 1889, Bismarck tried to ram a tough new anti-socialist law through the Reichstag. It would allow the government to strip socialists of their citizenship and throw them out of the country as enemies of the state. This time, Bismarck went too far. His action against the socialists was not only extreme but poorly timed. A new kaiser was on the throne, and he did not share his predecessor's faith in the Iron Chancellor. When the anti-Socialist bill stalled in the Reichstag, Kaiser Wilhelm II saw his chance. He maneuvered Bismarck into dissolving the government and calling for new elections.

Bismarck hoped for a new coalition that would back his policies. Instead, one after another of his supporters went down to defeat. Bismarck promptly resigned from the position he had held for nearly thirty years. Some rejoiced. Others wondered how Germany would fare without the Iron Chancellor's steadying hand at the helm of government.

THE KAISER'S WAR

Kaiser Wilhelm II was a self-absorbed man who lacked the temperament for affairs of state. Close associates considered him a spoiled child in a man's body. Author Michael Farr describes Wilhelm's idea of rule as "an endless series of dress uniform changes . . . military parades . . . and monument unveiling ceremonies."[1] The kaiser liked to wear medals he had not earned and conduct military maneuvers he did not understand. Wilhelm surrounded himself with "the crudest of military men, [who enjoyed] trading vulgar jokes and righteous arrogance about Progressives, socialists, and Jews."[2]

The Road to War

Wilhelm blundered his way into one international crisis after another. He angered the French by meddling with their colony in Morocco, the British by challenging the superiority of their navy, and the Russians by siding with Austria in a

dispute over Russian control of Serbia. His actions placed Germany in the center of growing unrest.

On June 28, 1914, Archduke Franz Ferdinand of Austria was assassinated during a state visit to the Serbian capital of Sarajevo. Amid threats of war, politicians and diplomats scrambled to make alliances.

A month after the assassination of Franz Ferdinand, Austria declared war on Serbia. After that, declarations of war fell in rapid succession. Europe divided into two camps: the Allies, led by Great Britain, France and Russia, against the Central Powers of Germany, Austria, Turkey, and Italy. World War I—the first fully mechanized war in human history—had begun.

This would not be a "good, old-fashioned war" complete with blaring trumpets, charging cavalry, and infantry marching in close-order drill. In 1914, armies trained for this sort of combat faced the horrors of trench warfare. Soldiers huddled in ditches, firing across open spaces at an enemy they could not see. War had become impersonal.

Fighting in the Trenches

The Germans expected a quick victory. They set up a two-front offensive, against France in the West and Russia in the East. The idea was to knock France out of the fighting with a furious assault worthy of Frederick the Great, then turn everything against Russia. To get at France, German forces rolled through Belgium, using brutal measures to crush all resistance. Terrorism was not a new tactic. Prussian general Karl von Clausewitz had recommended it more than a hundred years earlier. He, in turn, had borrowed it from the ancient Romans: "It is waste—and worse than waste—of effort to ignore the element of brutality because of the repugnance it [causes],"[3] von Clausewitz wrote. The idea was to breed such fear that panicky civilians would pressure their leaders to surrender.

Germany invaded Belgium on August 4, 1914. Soon, the Germans began a campaign of terror. General Karl von Bülow claimed that the townsfolk of Andenne had attacked his troops in a "traitorous"[4] manner. The punishment he ordered was swift and terrible. His troops burned the town to ashes and rounded up more than a hundred civilians to be shot in cold blood.

This was the first of many such reprisals (acts of punishment or revenge). In the city of Namur, Bülow's army took ten hostages from every street, warning the populace that they would be killed if any civilian fired on a German. This procedure was repeated in other towns, all along the way. To the dismay of the Germans, the tactic backfired. Instead of breaking resistance, terrorism made it stronger. Instead of forcing respect, it created deep and abiding hatred.

Mechanized Warfare

The old code of honor in battle had no place in the new trench warfare. The arsenal included everything from tanks and mortars to hand grenades and machine guns that "cut [soldiers] down like waves of wheat."[5] The Germans could mount long-range artillery barrages with cannons that fired shells weighing over seventeen hundred pounds.

In gathering eyewitness accounts of the Great War, military historian Francis Miller heard "stories more horrible than the nightmare [fantasies] of Edgar Allan Poe." Miller heard of men "buried alive" by explosive cave-ins, and "torn

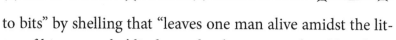

to bits" by shelling that "leaves one man alive amidst the litter of his comrades' limbs so that he goes mad and laughs at the frightful humour of death."[6]

Chemical weapons like "liquid fire" and poison gas added even more terror. Liquid fire was gasoline, sprayed from high-powered hoses, then set alight by firebombs: "It was like being in hell," said one veteran who survived an attack. "Some of the men began to scream terribly, tearing off their clothes, trying to beat out the flames. . . . None of us escaped that torrent of fire. We had our eyebrows and eyelashes burned off, and clothes were burned in great patches."[7]

Poison gas was the most dreaded of all weapons. There was no defense against it until gas masks were created. Deadly mist collected in shell holes, clung to the ground, seeped into clothing. It blinded men, seared their lungs, ate at their skin like acid. Those who inhaled fully died a slow and agonizing death. Poison gas became a symbol of all that was terrifying about mechanized war. "In the face of gas, without protection," wrote historian C.R.M.F. Cruttwell, ". . . the soldier in the trench [endured] torture and death."[8] In such a war, soldiers became victims; there was no room for "individual bravery, enterprise, and skill."[9]

This mechanization of death was not limited to the land. On the sea, Germany's new U-boats (submarines) "picked off cargo ships like bobbing ducks."[10] In the air, 400-foot-long dirigibles (lighter-than-air aircraft) flew bombing raids on allied cities. Fighter planes screamed out of the sky to make strafing runs (low-altitude machine-gun attacks) on every enemy position they could find.

Armies of the Reich finished with Belgium and rolled into France. Although the Germans won many battles, they

could not seem to win the war. Victory was no longer a matter of storming an enemy capital, capturing or killing the king, and claiming his territory by right of conquest.

In trench warfare, there was always someone left to carry on the fight. With long-range weapons, even small groups could hold a position against superior forces. The best Germany could achieve on the Western front was a standoff.

Meanwhile, the situation in the East was becoming hazardous. The German timetable had called for attacking Russia only after France was defeated. The Russians had other ideas. Instead of waiting for Germany to make the first move, they mounted a fierce attack against Prussia. The Russians soon exposed a weakness: the German Eighth Army, under General von Prittwitz und Gaffron, was disorganized and poorly coordinated. On August 20, 1914, Russian troops pushed through the Prussian frontier and captured the town of Gumbinnen.

The Chief of the German General Staff recalled Prittwitz and his second-in-command, General Alfred von Waldersee. He replaced them with Count Paul von Hindenburg and General Erich Ludendorff. These two men were destined to play important roles in Germany's future.

Last Chances

Paul von Hindenburg was a little-known general living in retirement when called to command the Eighth Army. He was a typical Prussian Junker, autocratic, grimly dutiful, and patriotic in the extreme. Erich Ludendorff lacked the aristocratic "von" in his name. He was a commoner who worked his way up through the ranks. This was not an easy thing to do in class-conscious Europe. He was also a master

strategist, confident in his own abilities and committed to victory at any cost.

Within ten days, Ludendorff and Hindenburg had scored an important victory. With Ludendorff supplying the tactics and Hindenburg the leadership, the German Eighth Army crushed the Russian invaders at the battle of Tannenberg. Within a year, Hindenburg became a hero of the German fatherland (a term for the German homeland). In August 1916, he was appointed Chief of the General Staff of the German armies. Once again, Ludendorff became his second-in-command.

Hindenburg and Ludendorff soon realized that Germany could not win with just a land war. Great Britain ruled the seas, keeping a blockade against all shipping bound for Germany. This was devastating to a nation that depended on imports. Germany's surface fleet could not break the British blockade, so Hindenburg made a daring move. He sent U-boats into the shipping lanes of the Atlantic. Their job was simple, sink everything that passed, regardless of its country of origin.

The submarines were the ultimate stealth weapons of their day. Moving invisibly through the water, they could attack and destroy almost at will. This tactic of striking any-thing that moved provoked a worldwide outcry. The United States in particular did not take kindly to having its ships blown out of the water. On April 6, 1917, after more than two and a half years of careful neutrality, the United States declared war on Germany.

For Germany, the gain of a new enemy was at least part-ly offset by the loss of an old one. The Communist revolution of 1917 knocked Russia out of the war in Europe. With no

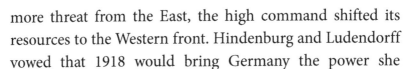

more threat from the East, the high command shifted its resources to the Western front. Hindenburg and Ludendorff vowed that 1918 would bring Germany the power she deserved.

The Price of Peace

In the spring of 1918, Ludendorff launched three offensives, each less effective than the one before it. The armies of the Reich regained territory only to lose it. They won battles only to stall in the face of enemy resistance.

On July 15, Germany began a desperate battle on the Marne River in northeastern France. Three days later, the Allies launched a counterattack. On July 18, French forces attacked the Germans and fought them to a standstill. By August 8, it was Great Britain's turn. Reinforced by troops from Canada and Australia, British armored divisions (tank corps) forced the Germans to break and run. Erich Ludendorff called August 8 the "blackest day of the German army."[11] The high command had to face a painful truth: Germany was going to lose the war. The morale of the troops was crumbling, and the Western front was ready to collapse. There was no choice but to ask for a cease-fire.

Foreign Minister Paul von Hintze believed that the Allies would be more likely to accept a cease-fire if the offer came from a new democratic government. General Ludendorff agreed. If a new government took the blame for Germany's surrender, the military would save face. At first, the strategy worked just as Ludendorff had expected. Like lambs going to the slaughter, the Social Democrats stepped into the breech. They pulled together a liberal coalition and presented the cease-fire request to the Allies.

To their dismay, the Allies were not particularly impressed by Germany's reforms. They wanted more than a few democratic reforms and a change of faces in the Reichstag. They wanted a complete transformation of German politics. A constitutional monarchy would not do; Germany should create a parliamentary democracy. Most stunning of all, the kaiser was to be removed from his throne. The new government had no choice but to agree.

Kaiser Wilhelm decided not to wait to be deposed. On November 9, he gave up the throne and fled to Holland. On the eleventh hour of the eleventh day of the eleventh month in the year 1918, the fighting stopped. The Second Reich, Prince Bismarck's empire of blood and iron, lay shattered at the feet of its enemies.

The German people were outraged. They had been led to believe that the Reich was winning the war. Had not Hindenburg's forces been winning battle after battle? Were not U-boats spreading terror on the seas? People did not understand that in mechanized warfare, it is possible to win the battles yet still lose the war.

They preferred to believe that the Reich had not been defeated. It had been betrayed. A "stab in the back"[12] from Social Democrats, liberals, and Jews brought about the surrender. The democratic leaders who signed the armistice were traitors. People called them "November criminals."[13] Their action was a stain on the honor of the fatherland. The German people, the volk, would not soon forget.

Public outrage opened the way for extremists to enter the political mainstream. These groups offered a variety of quick fixes and short-term solutions to long-term problems.

A SMALL GROUP
OF EXTREMISTS

In January 1919, the new German assembly met in the quiet town of Weimar to create a constitution. The Weimar Republic, as it came to be called, was doomed from the beginning. Too many Germans resented the whole idea of democracy. They felt it was being forced on them. Resentment soon turned to outright anger when the Allies imposed a harsh treaty on the defeated nation. The Treaty of Versailles required Germany to dismantle its armed forces, pay huge reparations (payments for war damages), and surrender great chunks of territory.

The German economy was shattered by the war; rising inflation crippled the country. At the end of the war in 1918, ten German marks equaled one American dollar. By January 1921, it was sixty-five marks to one dollar, and by July 1923, a ridiculous 350,000 to one.[1]

Somebody had to be blamed for this sad state of affairs. The favorite candidates were the November criminals who

signed the armistice, the Weimar government that accepted the treaty of Versailles, and the Jews. For German anti-Semites, there were always the Jews.

The Early Days of Adolf Hitler

The man who would one day rule Germany was not even born a German. Adolf Hitler was Austrian, born in the town of Braunau near the German-Austrian border on April 20, 1889. He was the fourth child of Alois Hitler and his third wife, Klara.

Alois Hitler began his life as Alois Schicklgruber, son of the unmarried Maria Anna Schicklgruber and an unknown father. In 1876, he was legitimized as the son of Johann Georg Hiedler, spelled "Hitler" on the child's records.

Years later, when Alois's son Adolf became supreme leader of Germany, journalists and political humorists had a field day with the possibilities of a führer named Schicklgruber. As Hitler biographer John Toland remarked, it is difficult to imagine "seventy million Germans shouting in all seriousness: 'Heil Schicklgruber!'"[2]

Alois Hitler worked as a customs inspector for the Austrian government. On the job, he was dedicated. At home, he was something of a tyrant. He made it clear that he expected young Adolf to follow in his footsteps and enter the civil service.

The boy had other ideas. In his 1925 book, *Mein Kampf* (My Struggle), Hitler spoke of his "profound distaste for the profession which my father had chosen for me. My conviction grew stronger and stronger that I would never be happy as a civil servant."[3]

After World War I, German territory was significantly reduced. Some Germans blamed the Jews for this loss of land. The Jews were also blamed for the country's poor economy.

Hitler did not become a civil servant. Instead, he became in quick succession a mediocre student, failed artist, and "street person" in Vienna. For a time, he scratched out a living by selling hand-painted picture postcards to tourists. It was during those days that he first became aware of what he would later call the "Jewish question."[4]

> Once, as I was strolling through the Inner City, I suddenly encountered an apparition [phantom; startling sight] in a black caftan [type of long coat] and black hair locks. Is this a Jew: was my first thought. . . . I observed the man . . . cautiously, but the longer I stared at this foreign face . . . the more my first question [took] a new form: Is this a German?[5]

This was the beginning of Hitler's obsession with the Jews. "Was there any form of filth . . . particularly in cultural life, without at least one Jew involved in it? . . . This was pestilence, spiritual pestilence, worse than the Black Death of olden times and the people [were] being infected with it."[6]

Hitler hated not only Jews but also the Hapsburg rulers of Austria. They were not German enough to suit him. Under the Hapsburg kings, "the poison of foreign nations gnawed at the body of our [German-Austrian] nationality, and even Vienna was . . . becoming more and more of an un-German city."[7] Many people enjoyed this international flavor. Hitler did not.

When World War I began in 1914, Hitler was determined not to serve in the Austrian Army. He petitioned King Ludwig of Bavaria for permission to join his army. The petition was accepted, and the twenty-five-year-old Adolf Hitler became a soldier of the German empire.

Hitler took well to the rough life of a front-line soldier. He liked the camaraderie of soldiers in the field, the sense of

purpose that enlivened the days, the feeling that any moment he might be called on to do something heroic.

He was twice wounded. Once, an exploding shell cut a gash in his thigh. The second injury was more terrifying; he was temporarily blinded by poison gas. These injuries were, to him, badges of honor.

Defeat, when it came, was a crushing experience for Corporal Hitler. In his fury, he blamed "Reds" (Communists), cowards, traitors, and Jews for what had happened to Germany. Something had to be done, he believed; and he was the man to do it. He decided to enter politics.

Building the Party

Nazism began with a tiny group of social misfits, who gathered in beer halls. In autumn 1919, a down-at-the-heels zealot named Adolf Hitler attended a meeting of what was then called the German Workers' Party. It was militant, nationalistic, and anti-Semitic. Hitler himself thought it was more like a club than a serious political movement, but he joined the party anyway. He received membership card number seven.[8]

To the ambitious young radical, the party was like clay to a sculptor. It was small and unformed, just waiting for someone to shape it. Hitler planned to be that someone. He took an active part in planning meetings. The others were content to meet in dingy little rooms. Hitler rented spacious halls and advertised the meetings in right-wing newspapers. In 1920, he changed the party name from the simple "German Workers' Party" to the more impressive "National Socialist German Workers' Party."

It did not take Hitler long to learn that hate mongering drew crowds. The meetings became noisy, boisterous affairs, balanced on the edge of violence. Hitler called for revoking the Versailles Treaty, creating a people's army, and excluding Jews from Germany's national life.

Hitler made his first major anti-Semitic speech on August 13, 1920. It was a two-hour lecture entitled "Why We Are Against the Jews."[9] Jews, he said, could not be judged as other men. They were creatures of alien and dangerous blood, doomed to corrupt everything they touched. The only defense against this peril was "to seize the Evil [the Jews] by the roots and to exterminate it root and branch. To attain our aim we should stop at nothing, even if we must join forces with the Devil."[10]

As Hitler's popularity grew, so did his impatience with the original membership of the party. Anton Drexler, the plodding toolmaker who founded the group, had become especially troublesome. Under his leadership, the party had been little more than a debating society. Drexler did not see it as a political force. He also did not like the rough, violence-prone ex-soldiers Hitler was bringing into the party.

Hitler decided to get rid of Drexler. He did this with a ruthless and well-timed maneuver. When Hitler felt sure the party could not do without him, he threatened to quit unless he was made chairman and given total control. With very little fuss, the membership agreed to his demands.

Hitler promptly did away with democratic procedures and began to build his own little army. He assigned Ernst Roehm to recruit and train a force of storm troops. Roehm was a soldier's soldier. He was brave to the point of recklessness, always eager for battle. Hitler biographer John Toland

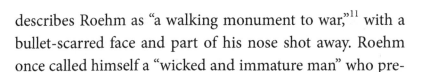

describes Roehm as "a walking monument to war,"[11] with a bullet-scarred face and part of his nose shot away. Roehm once called himself a "wicked and immature man" who preferred "war and unrest" to "the orderly life of your respectable [citizen]."[12]

The *Sturmabteilung*, or SA, quickly became a feared symbol of the radical right. Often called "Brownshirts" or "storm troopers" after the color of their uniforms, these handpicked troops were basically street brawlers.

The Beer Hall Rebellion

Just fifteen months after taking over the Nazi party, Adolf Hitler tried to take over the German nation. On November 8, 1923, storm troopers armed with rifles and machine guns pushed their way into a Munich beer hall, where the three Bavarian leaders were scheduled to speak. Hitler strode in behind them, jumped up on a table, and fired his pistol into the ceiling.

"The National Revolution has begun!"[13] he bellowed. The storm troopers took positions around the hall, guns at the ready. Hitler told the stunned crowd that no one would be allowed to leave; then ordered the three officials to come with him into a back room.

To everyone's astonishment, the men did as they were told. In the room, Hitler alternated between asking them to join his "revolution" and threatening to kill them. The prisoners were all aristocrats with the noble "von" in their names. They were used to giving orders, not taking them. They did not intimidate easily.

When Hitler realized he was not getting through to them, he used a favorite tactic. He simply ignored the facts

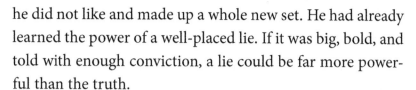

he did not like and made up a whole new set. He had already learned the power of a well-placed lie. If it was big, bold, and told with enough conviction, a lie could be far more powerful than the truth.

"The size of a lie is a definite factor in causing it to be believed,"[14] he once said. The masses were "a more easy prey to a big lie than a small one, for they themselves often tell little lies but would be ashamed to tell a big one."[15]

In his first lie of the night, Adolf Hitler tried some name-dropping. He boasted to the audience that General Erich Ludendorff would command the army of the new regime. In fact, Hitler had not talked to Ludendorff. The near-legendary general knew nothing about this strange little revolution or the role he was supposed to play in it.

Hitler's second lie was even more outrageous. Angered by the stubbornness of the officials, he locked them in the room and rushed into the main hall. Mounting the podium, he announced in a loud, triumphant voice that he had reached an agreement with the three leaders. Even now, they were in the process of forming a new revolutionary government.

Before the truth could be unmasked, General Ludendorff entered the hall. At first, he was furious that Hitler had used his name without permission; then he decided to go along. To Ludendorff, anything that might bring down the Weimar government was worth a try.

Duly impressed by this war hero, the Bavarian leaders agreed to cooperate. They joined Hitler and Ludendorff on the podium to announce the new regime. The crowd broke into cheers.

Hitler thought he had won the day, but he did not count on the Bavarian leaders having second thoughts. By morning, all three were claiming they had acted out of fear for their lives.

Hitler was not about to back down. At eleven o'clock on the morning of November 9, he led three thousand storm troopers on a march toward the center of Munich. General Ludendorff marched at his side. When they got into town, a cordon of police barred their way.

Nobody knows who fired the first shot, only that it set off a battle. One minute, the demonstration was noisy but peaceful. The next minute, everybody was diving for cover in a hail of bullets.

According to some accounts, General Ludendorff never flinched. The old warrior just kept marching as bullets whizzed past his head and bodies fell at his feet. Other witnesses said that he hit the ground at the first volley of shots, then scrambled to his feet and continued the march. Either way, Ludendorff did not retreat. He kept walking until the Munich police arrested him.

Hitler's actions on that day are also unclear. Some versions paint him as a coward who turned tail and ran at the first sign of trouble. Biographer John Toland offers a different view. He says that Hitler suffered a badly dislocated arm and was taken away by some of his men.[16]

Regardless of which story is correct, one thing is certain: The Beer Hall *Putsch* (revolution) had come to an unsuccessful end.

In Landsberg Prison

On February 26, 1924, Hitler, Ludendorff, and eight others stood trial for treason. During the twenty-four days of the trial, the eyes of Germany and the world were on the Nazi leader. Hitler took advantage of the publicity. The courtroom became a forum for spreading Nazi ideas. He ranted about the unfairness of the Versailles Treaty, the weakness of the Weimar Republic, and the unredeemed evil of the Jews.

On April 1, 1924, all of the defendants except General Ludendorff were found guilty and sentenced to prison. Although Hitler's tirades did not shield him from a guilty verdict, his ideas earned him a great deal of public sympathy. They also earned him a light sentence in a comfortable private room at Landsberg Prison. The sentence was five years, less six months for time already served. He would be paroled on December 20, 1924, after serving a total of sixteen months.

Hitler spent his time in prison dictating *Mein Kampf* to his faithful lieutenant, Rudolf Hess. Hess was also serving time in Landsberg for his part in the putsch. Although following Hitler had landed him in prison, Hess remained devoted. He firmly believed that Hitler was the best hope for Germany's future.

Rudolf Hess was the son of a prosperous businessman, but he had no taste for the world of commerce. He preferred studying political science and getting involved in right-wing causes. Before joining the Nazi party as its sixteenth member, Hess was active with the *Freikorps*, an anti-Communist militia. He later joined the Thule Society, a secret organization devoted to Nordic supremacy. All of these activities paled when he first heard Hitler speak at a Nazi rally in July

1920. It was a defining moment in his life. Hess said he felt "as though overcome by a vision."[17]

Hitler was the leader Hess had been looking for since his student days. While attending the University of Berlin, Hess wrote a paper describing his idea of the ideal German leader. This führer would be someone who understood the masses yet had "nothing in common"[18] with them. He would be both dictatorial and ruthless. He would not hesitate to "trample on his closest friends" and would command "with terrible hardness."[19]

Hess was not a brilliant man, but he was a loyal one. He was neither self-serving nor unduly ambitious. His absolute dedication to the führer made him content with a secondary position in the Nazi hierarchy (ranking of power and authority).

In Nazi terms, he was a visionary and an idealist. He was also emotionally unstable. In time, that would lead to one of the strangest episodes in the history of the Reich.

Starting Over

When Hitler got out of Landsberg in December 1924, the Nazi party was in disarray, and he was banned from public speaking in Bavaria. The Beer Hall Putsch had become something of a joke.

Unable to use his oratorical skills to rebuild the party, Hitler settled for backroom politicking. The publication of *Mein Kampf* substituted for the speeches he was not allowed to give. Party membership doubled from fifty thousand in 1926 to one hundred thousand in 1928.

During this time, the party not only increased its membership but refined its structure. It was like a miniature

state-within-a-state, with departments for everything from labor and industry to justice, science, and foreign policy.

A range of social organizations and professional societies got thousands involved in the Nazi way of life. There was the Hitler Youth for boys, the League of German Maidens for girls, and a National Socialist Women's Organization for adult women. There were professional organizations for such groups as teachers, law enforcement officers, and physicians.

To outsiders, all this organization may have seemed foolish. How could an upstart political party with only a hundred thousand members have a department of foreign policy? Hitler ignored the negative comments. He was building the Nazi party into the foundation for the future German state. He believed there would come a time when the people would be ready to listen. When that time came, he planned to be ready for it.

BUILDING
A NEW REICH

How did Adolf Hitler rise from failed revolutionary to absolute dictator of the German nation? It is difficult to understand the appeal of this intolerant, vengeful man. He was socially crude, poorly educated, and given to fits of rage. But he knew how to work a crowd and how to project an image that people would follow. Those skills would carry him to the edge of world domination.

Hitler the Spellbinder

Adolf Hitler was a natural orator. He had demonstrated this ability back in the Munich days, when his speeches packed rented halls. Even rivals recognized his magnetism. "Hitler responds to the vibrations of the human heart," said right-wing rival Otto Strasser.

> . . . [he is able] to act as a loudspeaker proclaiming the most secret desires . . . the sufferings and personal revolts of a whole nation. . . . Adolf Hitler enters a hall, he sniffs the air. For a minute he gropes, feels his way, senses the atmosphere. Suddenly

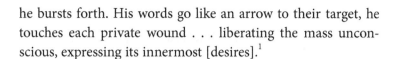

he bursts forth. His words go like an arrow to their target, he touches each private wound . . . liberating the mass unconscious, expressing its innermost [desires].[1]

There was something almost mystical in German ideas about leadership. Rudolf Hess had recognized this in his university paper. Germans did not want to be led by ordinary human beings like themselves, he wrote. They wanted "idols endowed with superhuman qualities"[2]—larger than life men with a commanding presence and big dreams. This was what Frederick the Great had been, what Prince Bismarck had been. This was what Adolf Hitler aimed to be.

"In Hitler, the prime German condition of leadership, of being quite unlike the led, found . . . fulfillment," wrote historian Richard Grunberger. "[He was] immune to what life meant to the average man, he was teetotal [drank no alcoholic beverages], vegetarian, a non-smoker . . . a man without family, without human ties of love or friendship."[3]

The worst mistake Hitler's enemies made was to take him for a strutting clown. His odd appearance, self-dramatizing behavior, and outrageous ideas made him a target for mockery. Silent movie great Charlie Chaplin made a wildly funny Hitler in *The Great Dictator*.

According to military historian John Laffin, many an English schoolboy sent his playmates into hysterical laughter with a Hitler imitation. The young "führer" would strut around with a pocket comb held under his nose, a hank of hair pulled over his forehead, and a fanatical glow in his eyes. "Heil, Hitler!" everyone would shout, their arms jerking up and down in "Hitler salutes."

The laughter was not justified. "There was nothing funny about Hitler whatsoever," wrote Laffin. "The man had no

sense of humour and the Germany of his time was a dark and desperate place, [full of] hatreds and prejudices, phobias and resentments."[4]

Seizing the Moment

Throughout the 1920s, the Nazi party remained small and relatively powerless. Then came the economic collapse of October 1929. The American stock market crashed, triggering a domino effect that shattered economies around the world.

The Great Depression, as it came to be called, was a disaster for the already shaky German economy. Businesses went bankrupt. Unemployment soared. Once more, the German worker was plunged into poverty by forces he did not understand. The Weimar government seemed paralyzed, unable to do anything to remedy the situation.

The Nazis stepped into the breach, offering catchy slogans and easy answers for the problems of the day. People began to listen. In the election of 1930, the party won 6 million votes (18 percent of the total), which translated into 107 seats in the Reichstag.

By 1932, German unemployment had soared to 6 million. In the elections that year, the Nazis more than doubled their share of the vote, with 33.1 percent. Their bid for power could no longer be ignored by the ruling elite; neither could their leader. On January 30, 1933, a reluctant von Hindenburg named Adolf Hitler chancellor of Germany.

Playing Politics

The new chancellor began flexing his political muscles as soon as he was sworn into office. Hitler knew that the old-guard conservatives distrusted him. He was careful not to

push them too far. He was also clever enough to figure a way around them.

His most immediate problem was dealing with the Communists. Having a right-wing fanatic as chancellor was more than they could stand. They called for open resistance, even for armed revolution. With a national election scheduled for early March, they openly opposed the Nazis in the political arena. Hitler needed an excuse to move against them.

That excuse came on the night of February 27, 1933. An arson fire destroyed the Reichstag building. The police arrested Marinus van der Lubbe, who was found at the scene. Van der Lubbe was a loner, a strange young man who claimed Communist sympathies but no longer belonged to the party.

Most historians and other authorities believe that the Nazis set the fire themselves, using the mentally unstable van der Lubbe as a dupe. Regardless of who or what caused the fire, it gave Hitler an excuse to go after the hated Reds.

Hitler claimed that the Reichstag fire was just the beginning of a Communist conspiracy to overthrow the German government. President von Hindenburg shared Hitler's fear of the Communists. He signed an emergency decree that suspended civil rights, authorized emergency takeovers of state governments, and gave broad powers to the chancellor.

Hitler dispatched truckloads of SA and SS men to round up Communists and throw them into prison. Many Social Democrats and other left-wingers got caught in the hysteria and were hauled off to jail. In a matter of hours, more than three thousand were taken into custody. Soon, local jails could no longer hold all the enemies of the Reich. The Nazis

built Germany's first concentration camp, Dachau, which received its first prisoners on March 20, 1933.

Squads of Brownshirts went through neighborhoods and shopping districts, tearing down Communist election posters and replacing them with their own. The old-line Nationalists joined forces with the Nazis. It was a right-wing coalition, born of shared fear and suspicion. Wealthy industrialists, desperate to protect their businesses, financed a lavish campaign.

Hitler went on radio, warning against the Communist threat. Even now, the Reds were preparing for a "blood-bath,"[5] he said. Only the National Socialists could stand against them. A vote for Hitler's party was a vote for a free, strong, and united Germany.

In case this propaganda blitz was not enough, the party also used strong-arm tactics. Storm troopers roamed the streets, terrorizing Communists, Socialists, Jews, and anybody who did not support Hitler.

The Nazis received approximately 44 percent of the vote. That was enough to make them the largest party in the Reichstag. But it did not give Hitler the two-thirds majority he needed to take over the government. To him, that was just a technicality. One way or another, he would get the majority.

Hitler could not pack the Reichstag with more Nazis, so he took another tack. He ordered large scale arrests of Communist members of the Reichstag. On the day of the vote, Nazi loyalists targeted the Social Democrats, preventing as many of them as possible from entering the legislative chambers.

The techniques were crude, but effective. On March 24, 1933, the Reichstag handed the Nazis what they wanted.

A two-thirds majority approved an "enabling act" that transferred legislative power to Chancellor Adolf Hitler. After that, the Reichstag was nothing but a rubber stamp for Hitler's policies.

The Fascist Vision

Totalitarian governments such as that of Nazi Germany are often called dictatorships or police states. Under an all-powerful leader, the state controls not only the economy and the government but people's personal lives as well. The press and the media are censored. Free speech does not exist. The state tells its citizens how to behave, what to think, and even what to feel. Secret police enforce the will of the dictator with tactics designed to terrorize the populace into submission.

The three main totalitarian states of the twentieth century are the Soviet Union under Josef Stalin, the People's Republic of China under Mao Zedong, and Nazi Germany under Adolf Hitler. Among them, these three governments killed millions of innocent people and enslaved many more. The only one that survived to the end of the twentieth century is the People's Republic of China. Although the tactics of these three dictatorships were similar, their goals were not.

The Soviet Union and Mao's China were Communist regimes (governments in power). The ideal Communist society is classless, without a distinction between rich and poor. Private property is forbidden. In theory, all citizens are equal, and the people own everything in common. In fact, the state owns it.

Nazi Germany was a Fascist state. The word *fascist* comes from ancient Rome, where the *fasces* (a bundle of rods tied

together around an ax) was a symbol of authority. The three most important characteristics of Fascist philosophy are glorification of the state, aggressive militarism, and elitism (rule by a "superior" class).

Unlike communism, fascism does not seek a classless society. Instead, a powerful elite rules the country, controls its resources, and openly considers itself superior to the common people. Fascists believe in survival of the fittest. To them, life is a struggle, and only the strong survive.

Elitism opened the door for racism. In the Nazi view, race and genetics [inborn traits] determined a person's worth. The Nazis idealized the tall, fair-skinned Nordics, or *Aryans* (a linguistic term that Hitler used to describe his so-called master race). According to the Nazis, Aryans were superior because they were born that way, just as Jews, Gypsies, and all dark-skinned peoples were born "inferior."

Fascism thrives on war and conquest. The Nazis believed they had a right to invade weaker countries, destroying their governments and enslaving their people. During Hitler's rise to power, one of his favorite themes was *lebensraum* (more living space) for the German master race. He planned to build a powerful military machine; then use it to conquer Europe for the German master race.

The Führer Principle

"To say that Hitler was ambitious scarcely describes [his] . . . lust for power and . . . craving to dominate," wrote Hitler biographer Alan Bullock.[6] Hitler was not satisfied to create a state based on Nazi principles. He wanted a state based on the führer principle.

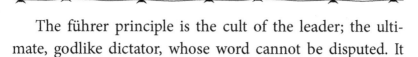

The führer principle is the cult of the leader; the ultimate, godlike dictator, whose word cannot be disputed. It was no accident of history that Hitler got this kind of power. He had planned for it all along. In *Mein Kampf,* he made his intentions clear. He would:

> free all leadership . . . from the parliamentary principle of majority rule.[7]
>
> There must be no majority decisions, but only responsible persons. . . . Surely every man will have advisers by his side, but *the decision will be made by one man* [italics in original]. . . . In no chamber and in no senate does a vote ever take place. They are working institutions and not voting machines. The individual member has [only] an advisory voice. . . . The [final decision] is [made by] the responsible chairman. This principle—absolute responsibility . . . combined with absolute authority—will gradually breed an élite of leaders.[8]

These "elite leaders" formed a rigid chain of command. Every area of society, from science and education to art and entertainment, had its führer. As absolute master of his particular domain, he set the standards for everyone else to follow. Underlings answered to him. The elite leader, in turn, answered only to an immediate superior. Officials could be as high-handed as they liked, so long as they remembered the one unbreakable rule: Final authority always rested with *the* führer, Adolf Hitler. To challenge him, or even to question him too openly, was to court disaster.

Baldur von Schirach, head of the National Socialist Youth Movement, explained the relationship between the individual leader and the larger hierarchy in his book on the Nazi youth programs:

> A single will leads the Hitler Youth. The [group] leader, from the smallest to the largest unit, enjoys absolute authority. This

means that he has the unrestricted right to command because he also has unrestricted responsibility. He knows that the greater responsibility [comes before] the lesser one. Therefore, he silently subjects himself to the commands of his leaders, even if they are directed against himself. For him, as well as for the whole of young Germany, the history of the Hitler Youth is proof that even a fellowship of young people can be a success only when it unconditionally recognizes the authority of leadership.[9]

Pomp and Propaganda

Adolf Hitler understood the use of ceremony, symbol, and propaganda in building his Reich: "He who would win the great masses must know the key which opens the door to their hearts," he wrote in *Mein Kampf.*

> Its name is not objectivity—that is weakness—but will power and strength. . . . One can only succeed in winning the soul of a people if, apart from . . . fighting . . . for one's own aims, one also destroys . . . the [opponent]. In the ruthless attack upon the adversary the [volk] sees at all times a proof of its own right.[10]

Hitler loved to stage enormous rallies. They were grand, showy events with blaring trumpets, pounding drums, waving banners, and thousands of uniformed Nazis marching in close-order drill. Sooner or later, every Nazi group had the honor of marching in a grand parade; Brownshirts marched, and members of the Hitler Youth and the League of German Maidens marched. The Labor Service Brigade marched, wearing military-style uniforms and shouldering long-handled shovels instead of rifles.

Nazi flags were everywhere. Giant flags served as backdrops for the speakers' platform, smaller ones decorated the lecterns, and regular-sized ones flew from every flagpole.

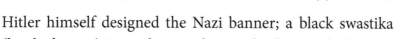

Hitler himself designed the Nazi banner; a black swastika (hooked cross) in a white circle on a background of bright red.

Many other symbols of the Third Reich were created by Joseph Goebbels, Hitler's Minister of Public Enlightenment and Propaganda. Goebbels's job was to glorify the Reich, all but deify (make into a god) Adolf Hitler, and Nazify the arts and the media. Goebbels gave the Nazis their marching song and their famous stiff-armed salute. He also gave them their first public book burning.

The man behind the Nazi propaganda machine was the most intense of Hitler's inner circle. Goebbels was born on October 29, 1897, to a strict Catholic family. In his youth, he was more interested in history and literature than in politics.

Physically, Goebbels was far from the Aryan ideal. He was neither blond nor muscular. He had black hair and enormous dark eyes, stood barely five feet tall, and had a crippled left foot from childhood polio. Goebbels used his nimble mind to make up for his physical deficiencies. He proved to be a skilled manipulator of public opinion.

Goebbels introduced the famous "Heil Hitler!" salute at the Nazi party congress of 1929. It was part greeting, part pledge of loyalty, part battle cry. The effect on the crowds was hypnotic. Constant shouts of "heil," accompanied by the raised-arm salute, fused a crowd of individuals into a single political machine.

Singing the Horst Wessel song also stirred public emotion for führer and fatherland. Horst Wessel was an early member of the Nazi party who got killed in a fight. There was nothing heroic about his life; nothing glorious about his death. Horst Wessel's only claim to fame was a song he wrote to honor the storm troopers. From this poor material, Joseph Goebbels created a Nazi hero and made his song into the official Nazi anthem.

In his effort to control German cultural life, Goebbels staged ritual book burnings. On May 10, 1933, in Berlin, books written by Jews, Communists, and other enemies of the Reich were publicly burned in huge bonfires. While flags flew, bands played, and soldiers marched, a crowd of Nazi loyalists threw armloads of banned books into the flames.

Like the Horst Wessel song and the Nazi salute, the book burning gave participants a sense of belonging to something larger than themselves. This fervor translated into loyalty to Hitler, volkish principles, and the Aryan racial ideal. As Germans affirmed that ideal, they also affirmed the racism behind it. In time, hating Jews, Gypsies, and other "polluters of German blood" seemed like part of the normal order of things.

The Enforcers of the Reich

The Nazis did not rely on propaganda alone to build their Third Reich. A vast network of secret state police existed to enforce government policies and ensure public loyalty to the Nazi party.

The *Schutzstaffel* ("guard detachment"), or SS, did not begin as a police unit. It was a small detachment of Ernst Roehm's Brownshirts, formed to act as an elite bodyguard for Adolf Hitler.

On January 6, 1929, Hitler placed Heinrich Himmler in charge of the SS. He built it into an elite corps that enforced Nazi racial policies, ran the concentration camps, and

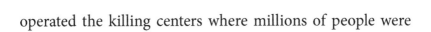

operated the killing centers where millions of people were murdered.

The SS men regarded themselves as forerunners of the new German master race. Candidates for the unit had to have an unblemished Nordic appearance and be able to prove the "purity" of their Germanic ancestry. They had to believe in Aryan superiority without question and be willing to eliminate "inferior" peoples without remorse.

The round-faced, bespectacled Himmler did not look the part of a fanatical racist. He was soft-spoken, polite in the extreme, and able to present the most outrageous ideas of the Reich in a calm and reasonable manner. For example, in a speech to SS group leaders, he openly called for utter ruthlessness toward "inferior" peoples:

> One principle must be absolute for the SS man: we must be honest, decent, loyal, and comradely to members of our own blood and to no one else. What happens to the Russians, what happens to the Czech, is a matter of utter indifference to me . . . . Whether the other peoples live in comfort or perish of hunger interests me only in so far as we need them as slaves for our Kultur [superior German culture].[11]

Born in Munich on October 7, 1900, Himmler was the son of a schoolmaster. At the age of seventeen, he joined the German Army, eager to find glory on the battlefields of World War I. He never got the chance. He was still in training when the war ended.

In 1920, he met Ernst Roehm and through him discovered the Nazi party. For the young Himmler, National Socialism was a perfect fit. He had what historian Robert S. Wistrich described as "natural snobbery."[12] He found Hitler's notion of a German master race irresistible.

Two years after taking control of the SS, Himmler decided to create an SS security service to hunt down dissenters within the Nazi party. He gave the job of establishing this *Sicherheitsdienst*, or SD, to a ruthless young man named Reinhard Heydrich.

Heydrich was a former naval officer who had been stripped of his rank for "conduct unbecoming an officer and a gentlemen." He had gotten a young girl pregnant and then refused to marry her. As head of the SD, he found his place in the world.

Starting with one typewriter and a small office, he built a network of informers. He gathered information on party members, SA leaders, and anybody who might oppose the führer. Some of this information was political. Some of it was not. Heydrich had a taste for scandal. He used hidden microphones and cameras to poke into the private lives of top-ranked Nazis.

While Himmler and Heydrich transformed a bodyguard unit into an elite state police, another of Hitler's close associates organized the feared Gestapo. Hermann Goering had actually achieved the hero status that eluded Heinrich Himmler. In World War I, Goering served in the German air corps. He was a daring pilot and won many decorations for his skill. After the death of the legendary "Red Baron" von Richthofen, Goering assumed command of the squadron known as the "flying circus."

As a genuine flying ace, Goering lent prestige to the Nazis when he joined the party in 1922. In Hitler's eyes, Goering personified the Aryan ideal. He was blond and blue-eyed, with a rosy complexion and an imposing physical presence. He was also flamboyant (given to showing off) and

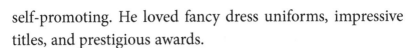

self-promoting. He loved fancy dress uniforms, impressive titles, and prestigious awards.

After Hitler became chancellor in 1933, he appointed Goering air minister of Germany and interior minister of the Prussian state. Goering made the most of his opportunities. One of his first official acts was to transform the Prussian state police into a new and more powerful organization known as the *Geheime-Staats-Polizei* (Secret State Police), or Gestapo for short.

The Gestapo soon spread over all of Germany. It operated outside the law, with authority to pursue "enemies of the Reich" wherever they might be found. The Gestapo did not have to wait for a person to commit a crime. Gestapo agents could arrest and question a suspected enemy "even if he is not about to be dangerous by a specific deed."[13]

Dealing With the Opposition

Hitler was relentless in getting his enemies out of the way. Any group that refused to join the Nazi program had to be rendered harmless. On April 1, 1933, he stuck a blow at his favorite target: the Jews. He called for a nationwide, one-day boycott of Jewish businesses on April 1, 1933. A week after that, he cut deeper, with a decree that barred Jews from all forms of government employment.

His next target was the labor unions, which he considered hotbeds of Communist and Socialist activity. He began by proclaiming a Day of National Labor to celebrate something that did not yet exist: unity between workers and government. On May 1, 1933, a nighttime rally drew an estimated several hundred thousand workers.[14] They listened to the führer talk about the dignity of labor and the need for

loyalty to the fatherland. By the time he finished, they were cheering and singing "Deutschland Uber Alles" ("Germany Over All").

The next morning, the SS and SA went to work. They arrested labor leaders, shut down union offices, and muzzled the labor press. By the end of the day, they had essentially wiped out organized labor. The rank-and-file workers were forced to join a new organization called the German Labor Front. Similar actions followed, bringing more sectors of the German economy under government control. Hitler replaced existing agricultural organizations with a new political group for farmers, the Reich Nutrition Estate. In industry, the Reich Estates of Trade and Handicraft replaced the old Chamber of Industry and Commerce. The Adolf Hitler Foundation of German Business brought big business into the Nazi fold and gave the government control of the marketplace.

The next step was to eliminate any remaining political opposition. On June 22, the Social Democratic party was outlawed and its members expelled from the Reichstag. On July 14, Hitler and his cabinet declared the Nazi party to be the only legal political party in Germany. By December, the party and the state were united, forming a new German Reich that was both a government and a way of life.

All that remained for Hitler to do was bring the military into line, await the death of the aged and ailing Hindenburg, and prepare himself to assume more power than any other German had ever possessed.

Chapter 5

ABSOLUTE POWER

"Power tends to corrupt and absolute power corrupts absolutely," wrote Lord John Acton in 1887.[1] Adolf Hitler seemed determined to prove those words. He wanted power and he would use anyone or anything to get it. He would also destroy whatever stood in his way.

The Night of the Long Knives

In the summer of 1934, Hitler's march to power hit a snag. Ernst Roehm had built the SA into a force so powerful it threatened the regular army. When Hitler was on the rise, he had needed street fighters and revolutionaries to run rough-shod over his opponents. After he became chancellor, his needs changed.

Ernst Roehm did not appreciate that fact. He still wanted a revolution that would destroy the existing power structure and give the SA total control of the German Army. That made him a liability to his former comrades in the Nazi party.

Hitler knew he could not build an empire without the support of industry and the military. The price of that support was his promise to curb the power of the SA. Hitler made that promise.

Hermann Goering, Heinrich Himmler, and Himmler's second-in-command, Reinhard Heydrich, spearheaded the plot against Roehm. They had come to fear the SA as a threat to their own power.

Roehm's enemies did everything possible to smear him. They made him out to be a traitor to the führer and to the party. They even brought out the best-known "secret" in the Nazi party: that Roehm and many of his SA lieutenants were homosexuals. Before Roehm outlived his usefulness, his homosexuality was something everybody knew but pretended they did not. Afterward, it was a "shocking discovery."

On June 30, 1934—a date that would forever be remembered as the "Night of the Long Knives"—Hitler gave the order to purge the SA. The SS rounded up Brownshirt leaders. Some were shot in the streets and some in their beds. The lucky ones were hauled off to jail. Roehm himself was taken into custody in the predawn hours of July 1. Later that day, he was executed by personal order of the führer.

No one knows exactly how many died in the purge. According to most sources, at least one hundred people, and probably more, were executed or killed during arrest. All of them died without trial, marked as traitors to the Reich.

For Hitler and his accomplices, the Night of the Long Knives was a great success. Even before the killing stopped, General Wilhelm von Blomberg made a formal statement of the army's "complete loyalty"[2] to the führer. Himmler gained control of the Gestapo as well as the SS when Goering made him chief of the Prussian Secret State Police. As Himmler's second-in-command, Heydrich assumed responsibility for the day-to-day operations of the Gestapo. Goering himself was shortly promoted to commander in chief of the *Luftwaffe* (air force).

A month after the Roehm purge, on August 2, 1934, President von Hindenburg died. Hitler immediately combined the offices of president and chancellor. This meant that he was also supreme commander of the *Wehrmacht* (the combined armed services of Germany, including the army, navy, and air force).

Cleaning Up the Reich

A structured, authoritarian society cannot function without political, social, and ideological unity. The Reich had no room for anybody who could not—or would not—fit into the Nazi mold. The process of identifying "undesirables" began soon after Hitler came to power.

As more people were arrested, the Nazis built new concentration camps to house them. In time, there was a vast network of camps, spreading through Germany, Austria, and into the conquered nations of Europe.

Homosexuals were among the first to be targeted for deportation to the camps. Arrests began in 1934, after the Roehm purge triggered a wave of homophobia (fear and hatred of homosexuals). Clergymen denounced homosexuality as a sin, college professors called it a moral disease, and doctors called it "a threat to public health."[3] All over

Germany, homosexuals and suspected homosexuals were rounded up and imprisoned.

Next came Jehovah's Witnesses, who openly refused to salute the Nazi flag, swear obedience to the führer, or serve in the armed forces. For this "treason," they were imprisoned. Witnesses who renounced their religion and pledged allegiance to the Reich could go free. Few of them agreed to do this. They stood by their convictions in spite of the cost.

Gypsies were another group who had no place in the grim world of the Third Reich. They were dark-skinned wanderers who valued freedom and had little use for authoritarian governments. They disrupted the social order and "polluted" Aryan blood.

In the early 1930s, the Nazis used existing laws to deal with "the Gypsy problem."[4] Local police could arrest and imprison Gypsies on a wide variety of charges, from burglary to loitering. Gypsies who could not prove German citizenship were expelled from the country.

Finally, there were the Jews. In September 1935, the Nazi party held its national conference in the town of Nuremberg. There they passed the first of a series of anti-Jewish measures that came to be known as the Nuremberg Laws.

The Law for the Protection of German Blood and Honor, which was passed on September 15, 1935, prohibited marriages between Jews and people "of German or cognate [allied; similar] blood."[5] Non-Jewish women of childbearing age could not work as domestic servants in Jewish homes. Jews were even forbidden to display the national flag.

On November 14, 1935, the law was expanded to strip Jews of their citizenship, their right to vote, and their right to

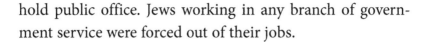

hold public office. Jews working in any branch of government service were forced out of their jobs.

The Search for Racial Purity

Nazi racial policy applied not only to Jews, Gypsies, and other "inferior" peoples but to Reich citizens as well. A broad program of "racial hygiene"[6] was based on the principles of eugenics, which was defined as "the science of the improvement of the human race by better breeding."[7] Eugenicists studied the process of heredity, the way in which inborn characteristics pass from one generation to the next.

To eugenicists, heredity is destiny. Many believed there is a gene for every imaginable trait. For example, one eugenicist claimed that a gene for thalassophilia (love of the sea) explained why "naval careers ran in families," and that "nomadism, the impulse to wander, was obviously hereditary because such racial groups as Comanches, Gypsies, and Huns were all nomadic."[8]

Such ideas may sound almost comical by modern standards, but at the time, nobody was laughing. Respected scientists all over the world took eugenics seriously. The movement was well established in Germany by the time the Nazis came to power. All they had to do was use it. In the name of eugenics, the Nazis justified everything from forced sterilization to killing "defective" individuals to wiping out entire racial or ethnic groups.

On July 14, 1933, the government passed the Law for the Prevention of Genetically Diseased Offspring, or Sterilization Law. People could be sterilized against their will if they had defects considered to be heredity. These included mental retardation, mental illness, certain neurological disorders,

genetic blindness or deafness, and chronic (ongoing, constant) alcoholism.

Later changes to the law allowed the government to not only sterilize people against their will but to do so without their knowledge. German historians Alexander Mitscherlich and Fred Mielke reported a case where unknowing victims were sterilized while they were seated at desks, filling out questionnaires: "X-rays from equipment installed under the chairs were . . . directed toward the genitals for two to three minutes, and sterility (as well as massive burns) followed immediately."[9]

An equally cruel method for mass sterilization was to inject an irritating substance into a woman's uterus. This would produce sterility by damaging the reproductive system. These injections were given during regular physical exams, so the patients did not know about them.

Dr. Karl Brandt, who participated in the sterilization project, noted that SS director Himmler:

> was extremely interested in the development of an inexpensive and rapid method of sterilization that could be used against the enemies of the German Reich, such as the Russians, Poles, and Jews. It was hoped thereby not only to defeat the enemy but also to [completely destroy] him.[10]

The Quest for Lebensraum

In early 1934, Germany began a rearmament program that was forbidden by the Treaty of Versailles. Working slowly and in secret, the Reich began building its arsenal.

On November 5, 1937, Hitler swore his military chiefs to secrecy, then announced a policy that would surely lead to war. The Reich needed to expand, he said. The only place to do that was in Europe, and the only way to do it was by force of arms. It was time to prepare for conflict. The question was not *if* Germany should fight, but *when* and *where* to strike.

Generals Blomberg and Fritsch begged Hitler to reconsider. Admiral Raeder did not think the führer seriously intended to go to war in the near future. He thought he was testing reactions, perhaps, or trying to prod the rearmament effort. The German Navy had no battleships. The army and air force had only minimal weaponry. "In no way were we armed for war," Raeder later said.[11]

In public, Hitler hid his plans behind a storm of words. He had become a master at the art of saying one thing and doing another. The gap between word and deed kept the opposition guessing. It was a remarkably effective technique.

When the Allies found out about German rearmament, they protested, but they did not act. Hitler pushed even further. At dawn on March 7, 1936, a small German force marched into the Rhineland, which was then under French control. Their official job was to reclaim the former German territory for the Reich. Their actual job was to test the waters of European diplomacy. Once more, the Allies protested but did not act.

Austria came next. Hitler's homeland already had a strong Nazi movement of its own. Thousands of Austrians wanted their nation to become part of the Third Reich. Austrian president Wilhelm Miklas opposed Hitler, but he lacked the support and the resources to mount an effective resistance. He resigned his office rather than preside over the destruction of his nation. Nazi loyalist Arthur Seyss-Inquart took his place.

On March 13, 1938, Seyss-Inquart signed a law annexing Austria to Germany. Britain, France, and other European governments protested but did not act. Hitler even managed to make the whole thing look legal, with carefully managed elections in both countries. The people of Austria and Germany voted overwhelmingly in favor of the *anschluss*.

Hitler's next objective was the Sudetenland region of Czechoslovakia. He proposed to annex the area for Germany on the grounds it had a large German-speaking population. Hitler approached this territorial claim with much caution. Czechoslovakian interests were protected by various treaties and alliances. He wanted the Sudetenland, but he was not prepared to provoke a war to get it.

He did not have to. None of Czechoslovakia's allies did anything to stop him. They were not willing to risk war for a little strip of territory of uncertain ownership. On September 29, 1938, the three governments that might have blocked the Sudetenland takeover—Britain, France, and Italy— agreed to Hitler's terms. The Czechs had no say in the matter. They could only stand and watch as the Sudetenland became part of Germany.

The Night of Broken Glass

Three weeks after annexing the Sudetenland, Hitler made a surprise move against the Jews of Germany. On October 27, he expelled eighteen thousand Jews from the country. They were born in provinces that had belonged to Poland or Russia at the time of their birth. Therefore, they were not German citizens. The government confiscated their property, and then hauled them to the border in overcrowded trucks, or herded them there like so many cattle. A Jewish shopkeeper named Zindel Grynszpan later recalled the brutality of that evacuation:

> When we reached the border, we were searched to see if anybody had any money, and anybody who had more than ten marks, the balance was taken from him. This was the German law. No more than ten marks could be taken out of Germany . . . . [The SS] told us to go—the SS men were whipping us, those who lingered they hit, and blood was flowing in the road. They tore away their little baggage from them, they treated us in a most barbaric fashion—this was the first time that I'd ever seen the wild barbarism of the Germans.[12]

After arriving in Poland, Grynszpan wrote to his seventeen-year-old son, Herschel, who was a student in Paris at the time. Stunned by his father's description of the ordeal, the young man vowed revenge. A German, any German, would do; Herschel Grynszpan was not particular.

On November 7, 1938, he walked into the German Embassy in Paris and shot the first German who greeted him. It was Ernst von Rath, a low-level embassy employee. In an odd twist of fate, Rath was being watched by the Gestapo. They suspected him of "anti-Nazi" attitudes.[13]

Rath died of his wounds on the afternoon of November 9. The Nazis wasted no time in denouncing the murder as part of "a Jewish-inspired world conspiracy against Germany."[14] The announcement triggered a night of wild violence all over Germany.

Mobs raced through Jewish neighborhoods; burning, looting, and killing. Firefighters watched as synagogues burned. Police watched as Jews were beaten and killed, and Jewish property smashed. "I was visiting my aunt nearby when my father came to get me," recalled one victim, who was fourteen years old at the time:

He was very upset for he had just seen freight trains packed with Jews. . . . About two o'clock in the morning, my uncle from another village knocked on the door. He told us Nazis had come into his village and arrested all the Jewish men. He hid, and later walked 25 kilometers to our home. My cousin, who was seventeen years old, had been tied onto a horse and dragged about the village. The two large synagogues in my town were burned.[15]

Similar horrors happened all over Germany. The attacks were supposed to appear spontaneous and unplanned. In fact, they were orchestrated by the Nazis. After Rath died in Paris, Reinhard Heydrich ordered the burning of synagogues and the destruction of Jewish businesses and homes. His only caution was to take "special care" that "non-Jewish establishments will be safeguarded at all cost against damage."[16]

He also gave explicit instructions about the arrest of Jews:

as many Jews, particularly wealthy ones, as the local jails will hold, are to be arrested in all districts. Initially only healthy male Jews, not too old, are to be arrested. After the arrests have been carried out the appropriate concentration camp is to be contacted immediately with a view to a quick transfer of the Jews to the camps.[17]

The devastation of this night was massive. The cost of the broken window glass in itself came to 5 million marks ($1,250,000).[18] From this detail comes the name *Kristallnacht*, the "Night of Broken Glass."

Sources differ on the damages, especially in the number of synagogues that were destroyed in part or in whole. One author says that more than one thousand synagogues were burned, seventy-five hundred Jewish businesses destroyed,

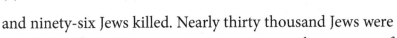

and ninety-six Jews killed. Nearly thirty thousand Jews were arrested and sent to concentration camps, where many of them died.[19]

Historian Saul Friedländer states that 267 synagogues were destroyed, 7,500 businesses destroyed or vandalized, and 92 Jews killed.[20] The Holocaust Museum and Studies Center of the Bronx, New York, gives the synagogue figure at 191.[21]

Whatever the actual figures, one thing appears to be certain: Kristallnacht was a crucial, horrifying turning point. Many historians regard it as the true beginning of what would be called the Holocaust. No longer would the Nazis settle for repressive laws and economic sanctions. They were ready to destroy and to kill. The Jews of Germany and the world had been put on notice; the worst was yet to come.

THE KILLING TIME

By 1939, the threat of another war hung over the world. In Germany, Adolf Hitler had become more combative; his speeches were filled with racist threats. Measures against Jews, Gypsies, and other "enemies of the Reich" became more severe and more public.

Hitler was ready to put the German people to the test. As he had said long before in *Mein Kampf,* "Those who want to live, let them fight, and those who do not want to fight in this world of eternal struggle do not deserve to live."[1]

One Conquest Too Many

When Hitler annexed the Sudetenland, he claimed to have no further designs on Czechoslovakia. He even signed an agreement guaranteeing the new Czech borders. It was one of his biggest lies. At 6 A.M. on March 15, 1939, German troops invaded Czechoslovakia. They met no resistance.

Hitler had browbeat the elderly Czech president Emil Hacha into signing what amounted to a surrender. Sign, Hitler told him, or Germany would invade. He threatened that Czech people would be killed, and Czech cities reduced to heaps of rubble. Hacha signed.

William Shirer called it "one of the most brazen [bold; shameless] acts of [Hitler's] entire career."[2] Once more, the führer had managed a bloodless conquest, gaining territory for the Reich without spilling German blood.

It would be the last time that bluff and bluster won the day. Hitler had finally pushed too far. Not even to avoid war would Britain and France give in to him again. The time had come for them to take a stand.

Through the summer of 1939, Hitler jockeyed for position. On August 23, he signed a nonaggression pact with Soviet dictator Josef Stalin. With the Soviets neutralized, it was time to strike. The führer set his sights on Poland. His generals, however, disagreed. Any strike at Poland would surely trigger war, and Germany was still not ready; steel, oil, and other important materials were scarce. The stockpile of ammunition would be used up within six weeks.[3]

Hitler ignored these facts. He was not gearing up for a long, drawn-out war, but for *blitzkrieg*, a series of overwhelming attacks followed by bursts of production. Each victory would feed the next. Factories would work round the clock, producing war material to supply the armed forces.

On September 1, 1939, Germany invaded Poland. With over a million men, supported by armored tank divisions, German ground troops pounded the Polish defenders. The Luftwaffe gave support from the air. Poland crumbled under the withering attack.

The invasion forced Britain and France to take a stand. On September 3, both countries declared war on Germany. Other nations scrambled to choose sides. Italy and Japan sided with Germany, forming the Axis Powers.

Britain and France formed the core of what would become known as the Allied Powers. France was knocked out of the war early, when Germany overran and occupied the country. Later, both the Soviet Union and the United States would join the Allied cause. The Soviets came aboard after Hitler violated his pact with Stalin by attacking Soviet territory on June 22, 1941. The United States got into the war after Japan bombed the United States fleet in Pearl Harbor, Hawaii, on December 7, 1941.

In the early days of the fighting, Germany seemed unbeatable. Nazi troops swept through Western Europe with terrifying speed. Nation after nation fell to Hitler's war machine: Denmark, Norway, Luxembourg, Belgium, the Netherlands, and, finally, France.

"Life Unworthy of Life"[4]

War did not distract Adolf Hitler from his obsession with racial purity. With a brief memo on his personal stationery, he began the so-called euthanasia (mercy killing) program. The deformed, the handicapped, the mentally retarded, and the mentally ill were its victims. Medical doctors were its most enthusiastic killers.

The euthanasia program started with newborn babies.[5] An agency called the Reich Committee for the Scientific Registration of Severe Hereditary Ailments pretended to be doing research that "would aid children with serious medical conditions."[6] To aid this research, family physicians, maternity

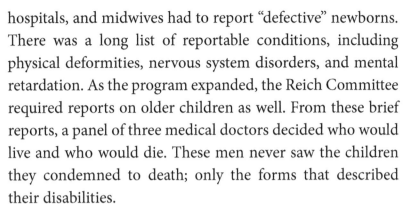

hospitals, and midwives had to report "defective" newborns. There was a long list of reportable conditions, including physical deformities, nervous system disorders, and mental retardation. As the program expanded, the Reich Committee required reports on older children as well. From these brief reports, a panel of three medical doctors decided who would live and who would die. These men never saw the children they condemned to death; only the forms that described their disabilities.

Parents of children singled out by these doctors were told that their son or daughter could benefit from a "new treatment program." In this program, the young patients would receive the finest medical care available and the chance for a better life. Few parents turned down such an opportunity. Those parents who objected, or who asked too many questions, were bullied and threatened until they consented. Parents did not have the right to choose; they had only the appearance of that right. One way or another, the child was bundled off to a "treatment center" in some remote part of the countryside.

A few weeks later, the parents received notice that their son or daughter was dead. The official cause of death might be anything from pneumonia to a ruptured appendix. The actual cause was more sinister: Their doctors murdered them. At the hands of these doctors, Reich Committee children died from lethal injections, poison gas, or starvation. One eyewitness told of visiting one of these killing centers. The director, Dr. Hermann Pfannmüller, bragged about starving his young patients to death:

I remember . . . the following general remarks by Pfannmüller: "These creatures (he meant the children) naturally represent for me . . . only a burden for the healthy body of the *Volk*. We do not kill . . . with poison, [or] injections. . . . our method is much simpler and more natural." With these words, he pulled . . . a child from its little bed. While he then exhibited the child like a dead rabbit, he [said] with a knowing expression and a cynical grin: "For this one it will take two or three more days." The picture of this fat, grinning man, [holding] the whimpering skeleton . . . is still vivid in my mind.[7]

In places like this, at the hands of people like this, at least five thousand German children[8] were killed because the Reich did not think them worthy to survive.

Once healers had been turned into killers, there was no stopping the search for victims. Institutionalized mental patients became the first targets of an adult euthanasia program. It was code-named "Operation T-4" after the address of its Berlin headquarters (Tiergartenstrasse 4).

To handle the large number of adult victims, T-4 established six killing centers. They were equipped with gas chambers disguised as showers and with crematoria for burning the bodies. These centers put death on an assembly line. They made it efficient and fast. The program officially ended in August 1941, after killing seventy thousand to eighty thousand human beings.[9]

Actually, the program did not end. Killings went on in secret throughout the war years and even beyond. This phase has been called "wild euthanasia," meaning it was unofficial and unorganized. Nobody knows how many thousands died in German killing centers after the euthanasia program had been officially discontinued.

The Ghettos

As the Nazi war machine rolled through Europe, Jews were set apart from the rest of the population. They had to wear yellow "Jewish stars" on their clothing and carry identity papers marked with a large *J*. They also had to live in specified neighborhoods, called ghettos.

The Nazis had planned for this from the beginning. In each conquered territory, they chose a slum neighborhood and surrounded it with walls or barbed-wire fences. Then they forced Jews from miles around to live there. People crowded into rundown apartments without heat or indoor plumbing. Lack of public sanitation made them prey to epidemic diseases such as typhus and tuberculosis. Food rationing kept them on the edge of starvation. Old people collapsed in the streets. Children begged bread from passing strangers. People who had managed to hang on to some of their assets sold or bartered them to buy unrationed food from outside the ghetto.

In the ghetto, there was only one way to survive: by working. The Nazis used the ghettos as a source of slave labor. Jews who became too sick or weak to work were sent to concentration camps. Nobody was sure what happened after that, but one thing was certain: People did not return from these camps.

Operation Barbarossa

By the spring of 1941, Hitler was planning "Operation Barbarossa," the invasion of the Soviet Union. His pact with Josef Stalin had served its purpose, and Hitler was ready to cast it aside.

Hitler's generals and advisors warned him against the Soviet invasion. It would spread German forces too thin, they said. Germany did not have the resources to fight on two fronts. The führer would not listen.

Even Rudolf Hess opposed Barbarossa, but he considered it his duty to help it succeed. He hatched an outlandish scheme to bring this about. He reasoned that peace with England would take care of the Western front and allow Germany to concentrate on the East. Hess convinced himself that he was the man to make that peace. On May 10, 1941, he made a secret flight from Germany and parachuted into England. The British quickly decided that he was mentally unbalanced and put him into prison. In Germany, the führer he had meant to serve condemned him as a traitor. Instead of becoming a hero as he had hoped, Rudolf Hess became a figure of ridicule. Everything he had worked for and wanted was gone.

On June 22, 1941, German troops crossed into Soviet territory. Operation Barbarossa was underway. Stalin immediately declared war on Germany and joined forces with the Allies.

Hitler was not content to fight Soviet troops on the battlefield. A big part of Barbarossa was dealing with the "Jewish problem." Units known as *Einsatzgruppen* followed behind the army. They had one job: to kill Jews and other "undesirables." The Einsatzgruppen turned mass murder into a precision operation. The largest single massacre of Jews took place on September 29 and 30, 1941, at Babi Yar ravine in the Ukraine. The Einsatzgruppen rounded up thousands of Jews and took them to the ravine.

Each new group was treated the same way. First, the Jews were forced to undress. The Nazis had found that people were less likely to resist if they were naked. The clothing itself could be sold or given to needy people within the Reich. After the war, a German eyewitness testified to what he saw at the ravine:

> When [the prisoners] reached the bottom of the ravine, they were . . . made to lie down on top of Jews who had already been shot. This all happened very quickly. The corpses were literally in layers. A . . . marksman came along and shot each Jew in the neck. . . . The moment one Jew had been killed, the marksman would walk across the bodies of the executed Jews to the next Jew . . . and shoot him. It went on in this way uninterruptedly, with no distinction being made between men, women and children. The children were kept with their mothers and shot with them.[10]

In two days, the Einsatzgruppen killed 33,771 Jews and filled Babi Yar ravine with their corpses. Sometime later, the Einsatzgruppen began using vans as portable gas chambers. They would load victims into the van, lock and seal the door, and then pump in carbon monoxide gas until everyone inside was dead.

At the peak of their efficiency, the Einsatzgruppen killed a hundred thousand people a month.[11] But that was not fast enough for Adolf Hitler. In the summer of 1941, he decided that the time had come for the "complete annihilation of European Jewry."[12] Another, more efficient, way had to be found.

The Final Solution

The task of planning a "final solution to the Jewish question in Europe"[13] fell to Reinhard Heydrich. On January 20, 1942,

he presented his plan at a meeting held in the Berlin suburb of Wannsee.

Heydrich did a thorough job. His plan dealt with everything from assembling Jews for transport to scheduling and routing the trains that would take them to extermination camps. These camps would be specially built for killing large numbers of people as quickly and efficiently as possible.

The Nazis built four extermination camps: Chelmno, Belzec, Treblinka, and Sobibor. They also added killing centers to two existing concentration camps, Auschwitz and Majdanek. Like the T-4 euthanasia centers that came before them, these killing centers were grimly efficient. They had gas chambers that looked like showers and ample facilities for burning bodies.

Barely a year after the Wannsee conference, the Soviet Army struck a death blow to German ambitions on the Eastern front. On February 2, 1942, ninety-one thousand German troops surrendered at Stalingrad. They were the battered remnant of a force that once numbered 285,000 men.[14] For the Third Reich, that humiliating defeat was the beginning of the end.

Even as the war turned against the Third Reich, the SS went ahead with the final solution. The death trains kept running, transporting thousands of Jews to extermination camps. Gas chambers and crematory ovens operated around the clock. Huge brick chimneys filled the air with human ashes, and everywhere there was the stench of death.

In an odd twist of fate, the man who laid out the plan for the final solution was indirectly responsible for its escalation. On May 27, 1942, Czech partisans assassinated Reinhard Heydrich. The SS used this as an excuse for brutal retaliation.

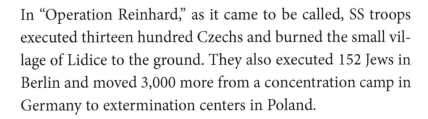

In "Operation Reinhard," as it came to be called, SS troops executed thirteen hundred Czechs and burned the small village of Lidice to the ground. They also executed 152 Jews in Berlin and moved 3,000 more from a concentration camp in Germany to extermination centers in Poland.

Reversals of Fortune

Reversals followed one on top of the other. By May 1943, British and American forces had crushed Germany's famed Afrika Corps and occupied North Africa. In Europe, the Italian Army surrendered to the Allies on September 8. The Reich not only lost its chief European ally, but also gained another enemy. On October 13, Italy declared war on Germany.

While the German Army suffered losses on all fronts, civilian opposition increased in German-occupied territories. On April 29, the Jews of the Warsaw Ghetto rose up against their SS captors. For more than two weeks, they fought in the streets of the ghetto. On May 16, SS troops commanded by General Jürgen Stroop burned the ghetto to the ground and executed any freedom fighters they captured. By summer, there was a revolt in the Bialystok Ghetto and inmate uprisings in the Treblinka and Sobibor extermination camps.

On June 6, 1944, British and United States troops crossed the English Channel to land on the beaches of Normandy (France). From there, they advanced with overwhelming force, pushing the Nazis back toward German soil. Soviet troops were closing in from the East.

Even while the German Army was retreating, the SS continued the final solution. A month before the Normandy

landing, the Germans began transporting Hungarian Jews to Auschwitz. By July, 437,000 Hungarian Jews had died in the "showers" of Auschwitz.

On August 2, it was the Gypsies' turn. In a massive killing effort, the SS liquidated the Gypsy camp at Auschwitz, sending three thousand men, women, and children to their deaths.

A Time of Reckoning

By the summer of 1944, many members of the German High Command realized that the war would be lost. Hitler did not agree. When his generals tried to talk strategy, he screamed and ranted about victories yet to come. Germany was in no danger of losing the war, he said. There were new planes being built, new offensives being planned, new "miracle weapons"[15] going into production.

The general staff knew better, but so long as the führer remained in control, there was nothing they could do. During this time, Nazi leaders faced an unpleasant truth about the führer principle. If the supreme leader faltered, the whole system could come crashing down. The Nazis began preparing for their inevitable defeat. In the death camps, the SS closed the gas chambers and shut down the ovens. In a desperate effort to hide evidence of their crimes, they destroyed Sobibor and Belzec in the fall of 1943. Chelmno was dismantled in the winter of 1944–45.

The SS fled before the advancing enemy. As they left the camps, they took surviving prisoners with them. On these brutal death marches into the heart of Germany, anyone who lagged behind was shot or simply left to die in the snow.

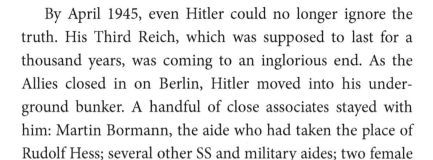

By April 1945, even Hitler could no longer ignore the truth. His Third Reich, which was supposed to last for a thousand years, was coming to an inglorious end. As the Allies closed in on Berlin, Hitler moved into his underground bunker. A handful of close associates stayed with him: Martin Bormann, the aide who had taken the place of Rudolf Hess; several other SS and military aides; two female secretaries; and Hitler's mistress Eva Braun. Joseph Goebbels brought his wife and six young children into the bunker.

Just before midnight on April 28, Hitler and Eva Braun were married. On the afternoon of April 30, they went to their private apartment. Nobody ever saw them alive again. Around 3:30 P.M., the assembled aides heard a single gunshot. Martin Bormann and Joseph Goebbels went into the apartment. Adolf Hitler was dead, sprawled on the sofa with a bullet through his head. His wife had swallowed poison.

The next day, Joseph Goebbels and his wife, Magda, killed their six children with injections of poison, then ordered an SS orderly to shoot them both in the head. A week later, on May 7, 1945, Germany surrendered unconditionally to the Allies, and the Third Reich ceased to exist.

Shortly afterward, the Allies captured both Heinrich Himmler and Hermann Goering. Both committed suicide rather than face execution for war crimes and crimes against humanity. Himmler took poison soon after his capture on May 23, 1945. Goering survived long enough to face the Nuremberg war crimes tribunal, which first convened on November 20, 1945. He was found guilty of war crimes, crimes against peace, and crimes against humanity. Two hours before his scheduled hanging on October 15, 1946, he

swallowed a cyanide capsule he had smuggled into the prison.

Last Things

So the war in Europe ended, and a stunned world came face to face with the human capacity for evil. Some 11 million people died in the Holocaust, 6 million of them Jews. This figure does not include casualties of war or the seventy thousand handicapped Germans murdered in the T-4 project. Though these numbers are almost unthinkable, many people believe that the most horrifying fact about the Holocaust is not how many died; it is how many did the killing.

The Nazis created a vast bureaucracy that involved thousands of people in the slaughter. Even when Germany was losing the war, the functionaries who scheduled the transportation, ran the trains, delivered the supplies, guarded the camps, and operated the gas valves kept right on doing their jobs. Without these workers, the Holocaust could not have happened.

Nazi leaders did not kill millions by themselves. Nor did they invent the "isms" that made the Third Reich an evil, murderous empire. Authoritarianism, expansionism, fanatical nationalism, racism, and anti-Semitism all existed before Adolf Hitler came to power. What the Nazis did was adapt these concepts to their own purposes and convince a good number of the German people to go along. The result was mass murder on a scale that the world can never forget.

CHRONOLOGY

B.C.

Germanic tribes settle Rhine valley.

A.D. 200

Jews disperse through Roman Empire.

400

Germanic tribes overrun Austria.

800

Charlemagne welcomes Jews into his empire.

December 25, 800

Charlemagne crowned Holy Roman Emperor.

1096

First Crusade; massacre of Rhineland Jews.

1618–48

Thirty Years' War leaves three hundred German states.

May 1740

Frederick II (the Great) crowned King of Prussia.

1756–63

Seven Years War; Frederick II expands Prussia.

August 17, 1786

Frederick II dies.

July 14, 1789

French Revolution begins.

May 1803

Beginning of Napoléonic wars.

October 14, 1806

Napoléon conquers Prussia.

1813

German states defeat Napoléon, reclaim the country.

1848

Liberal revolution in Germany brings reforms.

1862

Otto von Bismarck becomes chancellor of Prussia.

1864–66

Bismarck's wars of unification.

1867

Bismarck forms North German Confederation.

1870–71

Franco-Prussian War.

August 4, 1870

Southern German states join confederation; Germany unified.

January 18, 1871

Wilhelm I crowned kaiser of new German Reich.

1879

League of Anti-Semitism founded by Wilhelm Marr.

1890

Bismarck resigns as chancellor.

June 28, 1914

Archduke Franz Ferdinand assassinated.

August 1, 1914

World War I begins.

August 1916

Paul von Hindenburg appointed Chief of Staff of German Army.

April 6, 1917

United States enters the war.

September 28, 1918

Germans ask for cease-fire.

September 29, 1918

Germany agrees to form parliamentary democracy.

November 9, 1918

Wilhelm II abdicates the throne.

November 11, 1918

Armistice ends WWI.

June 28, 1919

Treaty of Versailles is signed by Allies.

September 12, 1919

Adolf Hitler attends his first meeting of the German Workers' Party.

July 29, 1922

Adolf Hitler is elected chairman of the Nazi party.

November 8, 1923

Beer Hall Putsch.

April 1, 1924

Hitler is sentenced to prison for the putsch.

July 18, 1925

Mein Kampf published.

October 29, 1929

American stock market crashes; Great Depression begins.

January 30, 1933

Adolf Hitler becomes chancellor of Germany.

February 27, 1933

Reichstag fire.

February 28, 1933

Hitler given emergency powers after Reichstag fire.

March 24, 1933

Reichstag gives legislative powers to Hitler.

April 1, 1933

Nationwide boycott of Jewish businesses.

December 1, 1933

Unification of German state and Nazi party.

June 30, 1934

Roehm purge (Night of the Long Knives).

August 2, 1934

Paul von Hindenburg dies; Hitler becomes both chancellor and president.

March 7, 1936

Germany occupies the Rhineland.

March 13, 1938

Anschluss: Germany annexes Austria.

November 9, 1938

Kristallnacht (Night of Broken Glass) begins.

March 15, 1939

Germany invades Czechoslovakia.

September 1, 1939

Germany invades Poland; WWII begins.

October 1939

Hitler authorizes the euthanasia program.

June 22, 1941

Germany invades the Soviet Union.

June 23, 1941

Einsatzgruppen death squads begin killing Russian Jews.

September 1, 1941

Hitler officially ends the euthanasia program.

September 29, 1941

Beginning of the massacre at Babi Yar.

December 7, 1941

Japanese bomb Pearl Harbor; United States enters the war.

January 20, 1942

"Final solution" conference at Wannsee.

February 2, 1943

Nazis defeated at Battle of Stalingrad.

June 6, 1944

Allied invasion of Normandy.

January 17, 1945

Nazis evacuate Auschwitz; death marches begin.

April 30, 1945

Hitler commits suicide.

May 7, 1945

Germany surrenders to Allies.

November 20, 1945

Beginning of Nuremberg war crimes trials.

✴——✴CHAPTER NOTES✦——✴

Introduction: Mandate for Murder

1. G. C. Kiriakopoulous, quoted in "Memoirs: WWII 'We had come to know fear and sorrow, but what we saw was beyond imagination,'" *Life*, December 1, 1989, p. 125.

2. Dwight D. Eisenhower, quoted in Brewster Chamberlain and Marcia Feldman, "The Liberation of the Nazi Concentration Camps 1945: Chapter V The Military," *U.S. History* (Parsippany, N.J.: Bureau of Electronic Publishing, 1994), n.p.

3. Calvin Goldscheider and Alan S. Zuckerman, *The Transformation of the Jews* (Chicago: The University of Chicago Press, 1984), p. 145.

4. John Weiss, *Ideology of Death: Why the Holocaust Happened in Germany* (Chicago: Ivan R. Dee, 1996), p. x.

5. Sebastian Haffner, *The Ailing Empire: Germany From Bismarck to Hitler*, trans. Jean Steinberg (New York: Fromm International Publishing Corporation, 1989), p. 216.

6. Weiss, p. vii.

7. Ibid., p. ix.

Chapter 1. Barbarians, Believers, and Tyrants

1. Tacitus, Germania, quoted in Norman F. Cantor, *The Medieval World: 300–1300* (New York: Macmillan Publishing Co., 1963), p. 54.

2. Norman F. Cantor, *Medieval History: The Life and Death of a Civilization* (New York: Macmillian Publishing Co., 1969), p. 199.

3. William Ebenstein, "Junker," vol. 13, *Colliers Encyclopedia* CD-ROM (Infonautics Corporation, Electric Library, 1998), n.p.

4. Anonymous French, in *Bartlett's Familiar Quotations*, Microsoft Bookshelf (Microsoft Corp., 1991), n.p.

5. John Weiss, *Ideology of Death: Why the Holocaust Happened in Germany* (Chicago: Ivan R. Dee, 1996), p. 71.

6. Ibid., p. 108.

7. Otto von Bismarck, quoted in Weiss, p. 80.

8. Alexis P. Rubin, ed., *Scattered Among the Nations: Documents Affecting Jewish History 49 to 1975* (Northvale, N.J.: Jason Aronson, 1995), p. 157.

9. Weiss, p. 98.

Chapter 2. The Kaiser's War

1. Michael Farr, *Berlin! Berlin! Its Culture, Its Times* (London: Kyle Cathie Limited, 1992), p. 116

2. John Weiss, *Ideology of Death: Why the Holocaust Happened in Germany* (Chicago: Ivan R. Dee, 1996), p. 125.

3. Karl von Clausewitz, *On War*, quoted in Seldes, p. 81.

4. General Karl von Bülow, quoted in Barbara W. Tuchman, *The Guns of August* (New York: The Macmillian Company, 1962), p. 314.

5. James Kindall, "WWI The Diamond Anniversary," *Newsday*, November 11, 1993, p. 80.

6. Philip Gibbs, "Story of the Hand Grenadiers" in Francis Miller, ed., *True Stories of the Great War*, in *Multimedia World History* (Parsippany, N.J.: Bureau of Electronic Publishing, 1994), n.p.

7. Philip Gibbs, "Story of the Evening of Liquid Flames," in Miller, n.p.

8. Quoted in "Works of Erich Maria Remarque: Biographical Note," *Monarch Notes* (New York: Simon & Schuster, 1963), Electric Library version, n.p.

9. Ibid.

10. Kindall, n.p.

11. Quoted in Sebastian Haffner, *The Ailing Empire: Germany From Bismarck to Hitler*, trans. Jean Steinberg (New York:

Fromm International Publishing Corporation, 1989), p. 114.

12. Haffner, p. 134.

13. William L. Shirer, *The Rise and Fall of the Third Reich* (New York: Fawcett Crest Books, 1962), p. 56.

Chapter 3. A Small Group of Extremists

1. John Weiss, *Ideology of Death: Why the Holocaust Happened in Germany* (Chicago: Ivan R. Dee, 1996), p. 228.

2. John Toland, *Adolf Hitler* (Garden City, N.Y.: Doubleday, 1976), p. 4.

3. Adolf Hitler, *Mein Kampf*, trans. Helmut Rippeger (New York: Reynal & Hitchcock, 1939), p. 17.

4. Ibid., p. 52.

5. Ibid., p. 556.

6. Ibid., p. 224.

7. Ibid., p. 15.

8. Ibid., pp. 57–58.

9. Toland, p. 103.

10. Quoted in Daniel Jonah Goldhagen, *Hitler's Willing Executioners: Ordinary Germans and the Holocaust* (New York: Alfred A. Knopf, 1996), p. 134.

11. Toland, p. 98.

12. Quoted in Toland, p. 98.

13. Quoted in William L. Shirer, *The Rise and Fall of the Third Reich* (New York: Fawcett Crest Books, 1962), p. 105.

14. Quoted in Seldes, p. 185.

15. Ibid.

16. Toland, p. 170n.

17. "Rudolf Hess," *The History Place*, 1996, <http://www.historyplace.com/worldwar2/biographies/hess-bio.htm> (May 28, 1999).

18. Rudolf Hess, quoted in Shirer, p. 77.

19. Ibid.

Chapter 4. Building a New Reich

1. Otto Strasser, *Hitler and I* (London: Cape, 1940), pp. 74–77.

2. Richard Grunberger, *The 12-Year Reich: A Social History of Nazi Germany 1933–1945* (New York: Da Capo Press, 1995), p. 84.

3. Ibid.

4. John Laffin, *Hitler Warned Us* (London: Brassey's, 1995), p. viii.

5. Bullock, p. 223.

6. Ibid.

7. Adolf Hitler, *Mein Kampf*, trans. Helmut Rippeger (New York: Reynal & Hitchcock, 1939), p. 449.

8. Ibid., pp. 449–450.

9. Baldur von Schirach, *The Hitler Youth*, quoted in George L. Mosse, *Nazi Culture: A Documentary History* (New York: Schocken Books, 1981), p. 295.

10. Hitler, pp. 466–470.

11. Robert S. Wistrich, "Heinrich Himmler" *Who's Who in Nazi Germany* 1998 <http://zelda.thomson.com/routledge/who/germany/himmler.html> (May 28, 1999).

12. Ibid.

13. Quoted in Thomas Robson Hay, "Gestapo," vol. 2, *Colliers Encyclopedia* CD-ROM, 1996), n.p.

14. John Toland, *Adolf Hitler* (Garden City, N.Y.: Doubleday, 1976), p. 311.

Chapter 5. Absolute Power

1. Quoted in *Bartlett's Familiar Quotations*, in Microsoft Bookshelf (Microsoft Corp., 1991).

2. John Toland, *Adolf Hitler* (Garden City, N.Y.: Doubleday, 1976), p. 346.

3. Robert N. Proctor, *Racial Hygiene: Medicine Under the Nazis* (Cambridge, Mass.: Harvard University Press, 1988), p. 212.

4. Henry Friedlander, *The Origins of Nazi Genocide: From Euthanasia to the Final Solution* (Chapel Hill: The University of North Carolina Press, 1995), p. 252.

5. Quoted in Alexis P. Rubin, ed., *Scattered Among the Nations: Documents Affecting Jewish History 49 to 1975* (Northvale, N.J.: Jason Aronson, Inc., 1995), p. 227.

6. Proctor, p. 15.

7. Quoted in Henry Friedlander, p. 4.

8. Charles Davenport, quoted in Henry Friedlander, p. 4.

9. Quoted in James M. Glass, *"Life Unworthy of Life": Racial Phobia and Mass Murder in Hitler's Germany* (New York: Basic Books, 1997), p. 43.

10. Quoted in *In Pursuit of Justice: Examining the Evidence of the Holocaust* (Washington, D.C.: United States Holocaust Memorial Museum, no date), p. 102.

11. Quoted in Toland, p. 422.

12. Zindel Grynszpan, quoted in Martin Gilbert, *The Holocaust: A History of the Jews of Europe During the Second World War* (New York: Holt, Rinehart and Winston, 1985), pp. 67–68.

13. Shirer, p. 580.

14. Gilbert, p. 69.

15. Quoted in Margot Stern Strom and William S. Parsons, *Facing History and Ourselves: Holocaust and Human Behavior* (Watertown, Mass.: Intentional Educations, Inc., 1982), p. 117.

16. Quoted in *Nazi Conspiracy and Aggression* (Washington D.C.: U.S. Government Printing Office, 1946, vol. 3), pp. 545–547.

17. Ibid.

18. Shirer, p. 583.

19. Mitchell Bard, *The Complete Idiot's Guide to World War II* (New York: Macmillan, 1998), pp. 59–60. "Kristallnacht" *The Holocaust\Shoah Page*, 1998. <http://www.mtsu.edu/~baustin/nacht.html> (May 28, 1999).

20. Saul Friedländer, *Nazi Germany and the Jews, Vol. 1: The Years of Persecution, 1933–1939* (New York: HarperCollins, 1997), p. 276.

21. Stuart S. Elenko Collection, Holocaust Museum and Studies Center, Bronx High School of Science. <http://voyager.bxscience.edu/orgs/holocaust/edguide/index.html>.

Chapter 6. The Killing Time

1. Adolf Hitler, *Mein Kampf*, trans. Helmut Rippeger (New York: Reynal & Hitchcock, 1939), p. 289.

2. William L. Shirer, *The Rise and Fall of the Third Reich* (New York: Fawcett Crest Books, 1962), p. 597.

3. John Toland, *Adolf Hitler* (Garden City, N.Y.: Doubleday, 1976), p. 543.

4. James M. Glass, *"Life Unworthy of Life": Racial Phobia and Mass Murder in Hitler's Germany* (New York: Basic Books, 1997), p. 43.

5. Henry Friedlander, *The Origins of Nazi Genocide: From Euthanasia to the Final Solution* (Chapel Hill: The University of North Carolina Press, 1995), p. 44.

6. Ibid., p. 45.

7. Quoted in Robert Jay Lifton, *The Nazi Doctors: Medical Killing and the Psychology of Genocide* (New York: Basic Books, Inc., 1986), p. 62.

8. Robert N. Proctor, *Racial Hygiene: Medicine Under the Nazis* (Cambridge, Mass.: Harvard University Press, 1988), p. 188.

9. *In Pursuit of Justice: Examining the Evidence of the Holocaust* (Washington, D.C.: United States Holocaust Memorial Museum, no date), p. 75.

10. Quoted in Ernst Klee, Willi Dressen, and Volker Riess, eds., *"The Good Old Days": The Holocaust as Seen by Its Perpetrators and Bystanders,* trans. Deborah Burnstone (New York: Konecky & Konecky, 1988; translation copyright 1991), pp. 63–64.

11. *In Pursuit of Justice,* p. 144.

12. Alexis P. Rubin, ed., *Scattered Among the Nations: Documents Affecting Jewish History 49 to 1975* (Northvale, N.J.: Jason Aronson, Inc., 1995), p. 232.

13. *In Pursuit of Justice,* p. 246.

14. Shirer, p. 1218.

15. Toland, p. 789.

GLOSSARY

anti-Semitism—Hostility toward, or discrimination against, Jews as a religious, ethnic, or racial group.

Aryans—Indo-Iranian ancestors of Germans on whom Nazis based their master-race claims.

Brownshirts—see SA.

concentration camp—A place where the Nazis "concentrated" prisoners in one place, treated them brutally, and used them as slave labor.

Einsatzgruppen—Mobile killing units that followed the German Army into the Soviet Union.

eugenics—An organized effort to improve a breed or race by management of hereditary factors.

euthanasia—Literally, "mercy killing." A Nazi euphemism for the deliberate killing of handicapped people.

extermination camps—Institutions built for mass killing.

Final Solution—Nazi code name for the complete extermination of European Jewry.

forced sterilization—Making barren; unable to produce children.

führer principle—Government by one supreme leader, who is often venerated by the people.

genocide—The systematic killing of an entire racial, ethnic, political, or religious group.

Gestapo—Geheime-Staats-Polizei: A secret state police whose job was to pursue and arrest "enemies of the Reich."

heredity—The way in which inborn characteristics pass from one generation to the next.

Holocaust—The systematic extermination of more than 11 million people, including 6 million Jews.

homophobia—A fear and/or hatred of homosexuals.

Nazi party—The National Socialist German Workers' Party.

November criminals—A derogatory name for the German democratic leaders who signed the armistice that ended World War I. Many Germans were disgusted by the treaty of Versailles and thought of those who signed it as traitors to their nation.

Reds—Communists.

Reich—German word for "empire."

SA—Sturmabteilung: "storm troopers"; the shock troops of the Nazi party, used to intimidate and control party enemies. Often called "Brownshirts," after the color of their uniforms.

SD—Sicherheitsdienst: A security service who hunted down dissenters within the Nazi party.

SS—*Schutzstaffel*: "protection squad"; massive state police organization that began as Adolf Hitler's personal bodyguard.

totalitarian government—A government that is ruled by an all-powerful leader, where the state controls virtually everything including the economy and the media, as well as its citizens' personal lives. Usually, a secret police enforces the strict laws the state creates. Sometimes called a dictatorship or a police state.

Wehrmacht—The combined armed services of Germany, including the army, navy, and air force.

zealot—One who is fanatical about something.

✴— FURTHER READING —✴

Ayer, Eleanor H. *Adolf Hitler*. San Diego: Lucent Books, 1996.

Berman, Russell. *Paul von Hindenburg*. Broomall, Pa.: Chelsea House Publishers, 1987.

Byers, Ann. *The Holocaust Overview*. Springfield, N.J.: Enslow Publishers, Inc., 1998.

Farr, Michael. *Berlin! Berlin! Its Culture, Its Times*. London: Kyle Cathie Limited, 1992.

Freeman, Charles. *The Rise of the Nazis*. Austin: Raintree Steck-Vaughn Publishers, 1998.

Haffner, Sebastian. *The Ailing Empire: Germany From Bismarck to Hitler*. New York: Fromm International Publishing Corp., 1991.

Heyes, Eileen. *Children of the Swastika: The Hitler Youth*. Millbrook Press, Inc., 1993.

Laffin, John. *Hitler Warned Us*. London: Brassey's, 1995.

Leitner, Isabella. *Fragments of Isabella: A Memoir of Auschwitz*. New York: Dell Publishing Co., 1978.

Mosse, George L. *Nazi Culture: A Documentary History*. New York: Schocken Books, 1966.

Pursuit of Justice: Examining the Evidence of the Holocaust. Washington, D.C.: United States Holocaust Memorial Museum, n.d.

Rice, Earle, Jr. *Nazi War Criminals*. San Diego: Lucent Books, 1996.

Rose, Jonathan. *Otto von Bismarck*. Chelsea House Publishers, 1987.

Stewart, Gail B. *Hitler's Reich*. San Diego: Lucent Books, 1994.

INDEX

CPSIA information can be obtained at www.ICGtesting.com
Printed in the USA
BVOW08*1032180614

356262BV00003B/16/P